The Japanese Iris

The Japanese Iris

Currier McEwen

Published for Brandeis University Press
by University Press of New England
Hanover and London

University Press of New England

Brandeis University

Brown University

Clark University

University of Connecticut

Dartmouth College

University of New Hampshire

University of Rhode Island

Tufts University

University of Vermont

Wesleyan University

Frontispiece. Partial view of Kamo Nurseries, Harasato Kakegawa, Shizuoka, Japan. Started as a family hobby garden over 100 years ago, it is a principal source of Japanese irises today. The family home seen in the background was built in 1773, the same year that Matsudaira Shōō was born. Photo by Mototeru Kamo.

Printed in Japan

∞

Library of Congress Cataloging in Publication Data

McEwen, Currier.
  The Japanese iris.

  Includes bibliographical references.
  1. Japanese iris.   I. Title.
SB413.I8M274   1990   635.9'3424   89–24974
ISBN 0–87451–512–2

5   4   3   2   1

As this book was nearing completion the group of advisors and contributors lost three of its members and the world of Japanese irises three of its leading figures: Dr. Shuichi Hirao, greatest of contemporary hybridizers; Mrs. Troy R. Westmeyer, founder of the Society for Japanese Irises; and William E. Ouweneel, for eighteen years editor of the society's journal, *The Review*.

This book is gratefully dedicated to them.

❀ Contents

☙ *Acknowledgments*

This book, sponsored by the Society for Japanese Irises, was written with the guidance and assistance of a Committee of Advisors and Contributors whose names are listed following the acknowledgments. These experienced growers of Japanese irises in the United States and Japan have provided information about these plants and their particular needs under the varying environmental conditions in the widely dispersed geographic areas where they are grown.

The aim has been to provide basic but not overly detailed information about all subjects of concern to the general gardener or the specialist, and to provide references for the reader who wishes more detailed discussion.

Special thanks are due to the following members of the committee who wrote the greater part of several chapters: William Ackerman—Hybridizing; Virginia Burton and Anna Mae Miller—Uses of Japanese Irises; and Leland M. Welsh—Shows. Eleanor Westmeyer provided many details regarding the history of Japanese Irises in the United States and of the Society for Japanese Irises. Florence Stout was the source of much helpful information about the early days of these flowers in this country. Ben R. Hager and Terry Aitken gave particular help on disease, and Adolph Vogt and John Coble on culture. Clarence Mahan, together with our Japanese colleagues, was our authority on the pronunciation of Japanese words.

Thanks are due also to Claire Barr for the section on where to see Japanese Irises, to Robert M. Hollingworth for information regarding pesticides and Agnes Waite for the rules governing awards.

Shuichi Hirao, Mototeru Kamo, Akira Horinaka, and Koji Tomino helped with much information on specific aspects of history and culture. The Appendix on Japanese irises in other countries was possibly only through information provided by individuals in those countries. Their help is gratefullly acknowledged.

We are indebted to the many friends who provided slides for the color plates. They are William L. Ackerman (plate 24), Terry Aitken (plates 12 and 19), John A. Coble (jacket back and plates 14, 29, 30), Donald Delmez (plate 23), Mototeru Kamo (jacket front and frontis, plates 1, 6, 18, 26), Jonnye Rich (plates 11 and 17), Alan and Dorothy Rogers (plate 16), Edward E. Varnum (plates 28 and 31), Leland Welsh (plates 10, 20, 25). Plates 2, 3, 4, 5, 7, 8, 9, 13, 15, 21, 22, 27 are from my own slides. We extend grateful thanks to Robert A. Bauer for his excellent pen-and-ink drawings.

It is a particular pleasure to acknowledge the generous financial help provided by individual members and especially by the auctions of the Southwest Michigan Iris Society, the Summerville (South Carolina) Iris Society, and the group holding the annual Northeast Beardless Iris Auction.

South Harpswell, Maine   C.McE.
June 1989

❧ *Advisors and Contributors*

William L. Ackerman, *Ashton, Maryland*

Terry Aitken, *Vancouver, Washington*

Robert A. Bauer, *Galesburg, Michigan*

Virginia Burton, *Ladson, South Carolina*

John A. Coble, *Galesburg, Michigan*

Jill Copeland, *Mattawan, Michigan*

Donald Delmez, *St. Charles, Missouri*

Chandler Fulton, *Weston, Massachusetts*

Ben R. Hager, *Stockton, California*

Shuichi Hirao, *Kanagawa, Japan (deceased)*

Akira Horinaka, *Osaka, Japan*

Mototeru Kamo, *Kakegawa, Japan*

Clarence Mahan, *McLean, Virginia*

Anna Mae Miller, *Kalamazoo, Michigan*

William E. Ouweneel, *Terre Haute, Indiana (deceased)*

Florence E. Stout, *Lombard, Illinois*

Koji Tomino, *Nagoya, Japan*

Adolph J. Vogt, *Louisville, Kentucky*

Bee Warburton, *Westborough, Massachusetts*

Carol Warner, *Upperco, Maryland*

Leland M. Welsh, *Kalamazoo, Michigan*

Eleanor Westmeyer, *Stamford, Connecticut (deceased)*

The Japanese Iris

CHAPTER 1 ❦ *The History of Japanese Irises in Japan*

JAPANESE IRIS is the name commonly used for the beautiful group of irises long identified with Japan, which has been brought to its modern state of magnificence through centuries of efforts by collectors and hybridizers in that country. In Japan it is known as *hanashōbu*. Its correct botanical name is *Iris ensata*. In the United States the name is commonly shortened to J.Is. Japanese irises are the largest of all irises, some flowers reaching 12 inches in diameter with lovely forms, colors, and patterns. They bloom about a month later than the tall bearded irises, and, unlike most irises, require acid soil.

The species *Iris ensata* grows wild all over the Japanese archipelago. It also grows naturally in Manchuria, Northern China, Korea, and Siberia where the species blooms somewhat earlier than in Japan. With the spread of farming and construction, many areas where the wild forms abounded have been lost, but many still exist.

According to Kamo, a leading authority on these irises in Japan, in ancient times Japan had no calendar and the farmers relied on seasonal changes to guide them in growing rice. The appearance of cherry blossoms marked the time to stop hunting in the forests and mountains and begin cultivating the fields. The iris bloom announced the advent of the rainy season, during which rice plants were transplanted from seed beds to the rice fields (Kamo 1989). In view of the importance this gave wild irises, it is probable that they were transplanted to gardens in very early times, but written records are lacking.

The book *Shugyobushu* by Jien (1155–1225) contains a poem that appears to be the oldest written description of Japanese irises in the wild. The earliest record of cultivated Japanese irises appeared about

1

five hundred years ago in the book *Sujyaku Ourai* by Kameyoshi Ichiso (1402–81). This told how a lord in Horikiri, now a section of Tokyo, sent his retainer, Kubadera, to the north, perhaps to the Asaka marshes, to gather irises. It is believed that in those days these marshes in the Miyagi Prefecture in northwestern Honshu contained some mutant types of *I. ensata* with colors rarely seen in the wild today, which were probably the basis for the development of today's cultivated varieties (Hirao 1988). The city of Nagai has a park displaying some fifty clones of Japanese irises that Shuichi Hirao refers to as the Nagai Old Variety Group, which are probably examples of collected wild plants. The form of the flowers is primitive, almost identical to that of the wild *I. ensata,* but they include almost all the colors and patterns seen in modern cultivars. Hirao believed that probably, despite the improvements introduced over succeeding centuries, the range of colors has not expanded beyond that of the original variants.

In Japan, Japanese irises are now called *hanashōbu* but until a century ago they were known as *hana-ayame* or merely *ayame*. The term is also used for the *Sibericae* which grow wild in Japan. To make matters worse, *Acorus calamus augustifolius* is also known as *shōbu,* a word which is also used frequently as a contraction of *hanashōbu*. Certainly this nomenclature has been very confusing, but today *hanashōbu* refers only to the Japanese iris *I. ensata* and its thousands of descendants.

In 1681 the book *Kadan-Komoku* (Outline of flower garden) classified irises by color and described methods of cultivation. The plants discussed may be assumed to have been chiefly collected examples of *I. ensata,* resulting from natural mutations. Such different colors as white, violet and purple were mentioned, as well as different textures and numbers of petals. Another gardening manual, *Kadan-chikin-sho* (Concise flower gardening) published in 1694 described eight varieties; a revision published some ten years later described more than forty; and by 1799 another manual states "The varieties, of which there are several hundred, are too numerous to record here" (Hirao 1988). Clearly, during those years interest was keen and a great number of varieties were developed in a relatively short time. However, the greatest advances came through the achievements of Matsudaira Shōō.*

*In this book, Japanese personal names are shown in the western fashion with the given name first and the family name second, rather than in the Japanese way with the family name first. An exception is made here in the case of Matsudaira Shōō. His given name was Sadatomo but he preferred to call himself Shōō, a name he adopted in his later years from *shō,* taken from *hanashōbu,* and *ō* meaning old man. The name has served as a token of respect ever since.

Matsudaira lived from 1773 to 1856. Hirao (1988), who states that he can, without exaggeration, be said to have brought Japanese irises to the highest point of their development, quotes from a biographical account of his sixty years of growing irises: "His father Sadahiro obtained wild specimens from all over the country and raised them from seed, but produced nothing unusual. Subsequently he planted some seeds which, according to the friend who sent them, came from the *hanashōbu* of the Asaka marshes, and obtained single flowers of a deep purple. He continued to raise seedlings, and by the third or fourth generation had obtained a large double bloom of beautiful color" (40). Matsudaira Shōō continued his father's interest, creating more than a hundred superior new varieties. He too obtained plants gathered in the Asaka marshes, deep purple doubles and light purple singles, which he used as parent plants. Since a large number of cultivated varieties were already available by Matsudaira Shōō's time, it is probable that he used them as well. His ideal Japanese iris was one with rounded, overlapping petals of comparatively flat form, thick, with velvety texture, good color and distinctive appearance. He disliked flowers with thin, drooping petals. "The iris is properly speaking a single bloom," he wrote, "and a good single cannot be beaten. Flowers with six petals or more are striking but they lack the dignity of the single variety. However, both single and double varieties are so taken for granted by now that it would take a bloom like a peony to really arouse people's curiosity." Years later he did succeed in producing such a peony type. In his words, "For several decades I had been struggling to produce the flower of my dreams and finally, it seems, man's efforts and the efforts of the maker of the universe coincided, and the rare flower made its appearance" (Hirao 1988, 41). It is probable that some cultivars still grown today were developed by Matsudaira Shōō. These include "Uchu," "Renjou-no-tama," and "Tsuru-no-kegoromo." Color photographs of these are shown in plates 35, 45, and 125 respectively of the monumental book *The Japanese Iris: Its History, Varieties, and Cultivation* by Motogirou Kuribayashi and Shuichi Hirao (1971).

During this period there were, of course, others growing Japanese irises, including Rakuo Shirakawa, Rokusaburo Mannen, and a farmer named Izaemon who started cultivating them in the Horikiri area of Tokyo. Mannen, who was given plants by Matsudaira, was particularly active and successful. Hirao (1988) states that together Matsudaira and Mannen "can be credited with having brought the cultivated Japanese irises to perfection. Since their time countless other varieties have been created by innumerable breeders but there has been almost no progress in basic features such as range of color or variety of shape—a sign, most likely, of the limitations imposed by the fact that all *hana-shōbu* belong to a single species" (41).

Following the long period of civil strife that ended with the Meiji restoration in 1868, the culture of Japanese irises in the Horikiri area of Tokyo, which had been considerable for several centuries, was resumed with renewed vigor. A number of famous gardens dating from the seventeenth and eighteenth centuries flourished there, as well as in other places. Admission was charged to view the irises, which were grown in paddy fields. One of the oldest gardens was the Kotaka-en in Horikiri, followed later by the Musashi-en, the Yoshino-en, and others. The Kotaka-en, in 1877, was the first to export Japanese irises to the United States commercially (Tomino 1963). The Yoyogi Garden, now the Inner Garden of the Meiji Shrine, was enlarged to include an extensive *hanashōbu* planting, and the experimental laboratory of the Kanagawa Prefecture started a *hanashōbu* breeding program which developed more than three hundred varieties. These and other gardens are described in an excellent article by George M. Reed (1931).

While these developments were taking place in the area around Tokyo, there were also very important developments occurring in the Ise-Matsuzaka district of central Honshu, and in Higo, an old province in the southern island of Kyushu. The particular Japanese irises developed in these programs became known as the Ise and Higo types. Until these names came into use, the numerous cultivars that had been developed over several hundred years through collection of variants and hybridizing in the area near Tokyo were all known merely as *hanashōbu*. With the appearance and naming of the Ise and Higo types, a similar sort of designation became necessary to distinguish the older ones, and in the 1920s they became known as the Edo type after the old name of Tokyo. Whereas the Ise and Higo groups are each more or less uniform in the characteristics of their flowers and were designed for culture in pots that could be taken indoors at bloom time, the Edo group was developed in fields and paddies over a very much longer period and shows greater variation in size, color, and other features.

During World War II most of the gardens mentioned above were given up. In addition, many varieties of irises were lost in the severe floods of 1947. Fortunately, one hundred or more were saved through the efforts of Wasaburou Gotou and others and were planted in the Inner Garden of the Meiji Shrine in Tokyo.

The Ise Japanese Iris

Ise, some fifty miles southeast of Kyoto, is the site of the grand shrines to the ancestors of the Imperial Family and has close ties to Kyoto, the former capital of Japan. Since the seventeenth century its shrines have been an object of pilgrimage, and today it is also a tourist attraction.

Although the early history of the development of the Ise *hanashōbu* is uncertain because of the meager records of those times, genetic differences between them and the Edo and Higo strains suggest that at least some of them were derived from wild forms different from those of the Asaka marshes. It is believed that Sadagoro Yoshii (1776–1869) was the originator of the Ise type. He selected existing varieties and improved them through his own breeding program, and his efforts were continued by such men as Saikichi Noguchi (1829–1910) and Kenzaburo Nagabayashi (1876–1937). On the death of Yoshii his son gave his plants to Noguchi. Others developing improved Ise *hanashōbu* were Kenjiro Izeki, his nephew Mankichi Tsuyoshigawa, and Taisuki Hirode. Sukeichi Miyagawa, head of the Mie Prefectural Agricultural Laboratory, who also worked to improve these irises, was the first to use the name Ise *hanashōbu* for them, about 1910.

More recently the Ise-Japanese irises have been the particular interest of Koji Tomino who has done much to preserve the older Ise varieties and improve them through his hybridizing efforts. Currently there are some forty of the traditional varieties and more than two hundred more modern ones. The characteristics of the Ise irises are governed by very strict rules, which are discussed in chapters 3 and 4 as are also those of the Edo and Higo types.

The Higo Japanese Iris

The Higo strain is a direct descendant of the Edo group, produced by interbreeding successive generations of selected Edo varieties. Higo, an old province in Kyushu corresponding to the present Kumamoto Prefecture, has been an important horticultural center since ancient times. In 1833 Lord Hosokawa, ruler of a feudal clan there, arranged for one of his retainers, Junnosuke Yoshida, to work with Matsudaira Shōō in Edo. By 1852 Yoshida had brought back to Higo some sixty-four Edo varieties. With the encouragement of Lord Hosokawa, an intensive hybridizing program developed. Hirao (1988) writes "a number of groups of iris growers grew up which engaged in lively competition with each other and developed large numbers of new varieties. Each group jealously guarded its own seedlings, which were not allowed to pass into the hands of anyone outside the group, not even to relatives" (44).

In 1886 these individual groups were brought together in the *Man-getsu-kai* (Full Moon Society), devoted to the growing and improvement of Higo irises. This society was reorganized and strengthened in 1893. Among the hybridizers who contributed to the development of the Higo irises from the late 1800s to the mid 1900s were Tamegorou Miyake, Isaburou Hayashi, Kadoyoshi Koyama, Matatarou Tomita, Tadatsugu Kouda, Nobutsune Nishida, Togiro Seto, and Issei Nishida.

Hirao has explained that for a number of reasons—the special love of the people of Kumamoto for the iris, their fear of having their plants stolen, and the frequency of heavy rain at bloom time in that area—the Higo irises came to be grown in pots. The pot culture of chrysanthemums and morning glories was already being practiced, and techniques for growing the irises in pots developed rapidly. Rules along the lines of the tea ceremony and the old schools of flower arrangement were gradually developed for displaying the plants inside the house. The plants in their pots were displayed in front of a gold screen, a setting in which flowers of pure white or of rich single colors are more beautiful than those with pale colors or patterns. This naturally led to hybridizing efforts for the desired types. Displaying the plants indoors also discouraged efforts to develop branching, since the ideal for display was one magnificent bloom. In recent years the trend has been more and more to grow the Higos out of doors and, as a result, they have now developed in a wide variety of colors and patterns and with good branching and bud count.

The name Higo *hanashōbu* came into use in the 1860s. In 1914 the name was changed to Kumamoto *hanashōbu* (Tomino 1963) but the term Higo continues in general use.

In the one hundred thirty-eight years between the time the Edo irises were first taken to Kumamoto in 1833 and 1971, some ninety-three hybridizers in Japan alone developed a total of 1,170 new Higo cultivars (Hirao 1988). Originally the jealous guarding of the Higo irises from outside the group made it extremely difficult to obtain them, but in 1914 Nobutsune Nishida (1862–1938) began to sell them and even to export them to Europe and the United States. In addition, he developed a large number of new varieties, but unfortunately all but approximately fifty of these plants were lost during World War II. Since the war Nishida's work has been carried on by Shuichi Hirao, Yoshio Mitsuda, Shigeo Oshida, Mototeru Kamo, and others, and a large number of new and improved cultivars has been produced. Similar renewed efforts have been made with the Edo and Ise irises. Shichiro Maeda and especially Koji Tomino have worked intensively to develop new, improved varieties of Ise irises. The late Shuichi Hirao, who is recognized by all as the world's leading recent hybridizer of Japanese irises, used all three groups, as do most other hybridizers. Thus, the differences that distinguished the groups in the past have become less sharp, and this trend will probably continue with further interbreeding.

It is good to know that the tradition of centuries of devoted work for the advancement and improvement of Japanese iris continues unabated in the country in which it began.

Current activities and the societies in Japan concerned with Japanese irises are discussed in appendix A.

CHAPTER 2 🌿 *The History of Japanese Irises in the United States*

COMPARED WITH five hundred years of active interest in Japan, the history of Japanese irises in the United States is short indeed. It is believed that the first varieties were imported by Thomas Hogg, Jr., about the year 1869 (Cameron 1908). Thomas Hogg, Sr., owned an important commercial nursery in New York City. His son was highly regarded and active in civic affairs. When Japan was opened by Admiral Perry to foreign business in 1853, agents were appointed to work with the Japanese in the development of a customs service there. Thomas Hogg, Jr., was appointed by President Lincoln in 1862 to serve as one of these marshals. He remained in Japan for eight years, during which time he studied plants native to Japan and sent many to the family nursery in New York. In view of the importance of Japanese irises in Japan, it has been assumed that they were among those he introduced into the United States. We have not succeeded in finding a catalog of the Hogg nursery but a copy of the wholesale catalog of Woolson and Company, Passaic, New Jersey, for 1879 states "We offer seedlings from the best European stocks, and also named varieties from the stock originally introduced from Japan by Mr. Thomas Hogg." It is interesting to note that in his later years Hogg was chairman of the committee of influential men and women who brought about the establishment of the world-famous New York Botanical Garden in the Bronx.

Cameron (1908) goes on to say that it took many years for Japanese irises to become popular but by 1908 they were to be found in almost every garden. Reed, writing in 1928, agrees that Hogg was the first to introduce them in this country and comments on their wide distribution and development, which he attributes in part to the large number of seedlings raised. Extremely important also in the spread of Japanese irises in those early days were the commercial growers who became interested in them. In addition to Woolson and Company, by 1885 V. H. Hallock, Son & Thorp of Queens, New York, was also importing them. Hallock introduced and promoted at least fifteen varieties in the United States. Among these the rich brownish-red "Mahogany" of 1893 was sensational and was still being used some thirty years later by Arlie Payne in his breeding; and the lovely white "Gold Bound" so impressed Arthur Hazzard that he used it as a parent in his early crosses. The Hallock nursery, which was bought by John Louis Childs who increased his planting on Long Island at what was called Flowerfields to twenty acres by 1920, had at its peak some four hundred different varieties. Childs continued the introduction of new varieties, some of which were his own hybrids. Some of these, such as "La Favorite," are still being sold.

A number of nurseries and firms in Japan supplied plants to American growers. A very important one of these was the Yokohama Nursery Co., one of the few Japanese nurseries then selling retail in the United States, which had an office in New York as well as in Yokohama. Before 1909 it was perhaps the chief source of Japanese irises grown in this country, and also shipped large quantities of seeds that were undoubtedly the source of early seedlings named by American growers.

Firms in other countries serving the American market included Barr and Sons and Wallace and Company in England, Vilmorin et Cie in Paris, and Alfred Unger in Germany. Hallock had depended on European firms for most of his imports. Other early American nurseries that imported Japanese irises included Leonard Joerg of New Hyde Park, New York, about 1870; Samuel G. Harris of Rosedale Nurseries, Tarrytown, New York; J. F. Lovett of Little Silver, New Jersey (which also had the distinction of introducing many of the named rose seedlings of that famous hybridizer Dr. Walter Van Fleet); Henry A. Dreer of Philadelphia who began selling Japanese irises in 1872; Andora Nurseries also in Philadelphia; and R. & J. Farquhar Co. of Boston. It is interesting to note that the spring 1897 catalog of the Storrs and Harrison Company of Painesville, Ohio, offered "6 kaempheri iris, all double flowered, for 15¢ each or 4 for 50¢"!

After the turn of the century the number of nurseries and individuals growing and hybridizing Japanese irises increased rapidly. The well-known hybridizer Bertram Farr of Wyomissing, Pennsylvania, offered his first catalog in 1908 and in 1920 reported the import of a collection of Japanese irises "duplicating those in the garden of the Mikado." Lovett, mentioned above, introduced "Prof. Geogeson" in 1902 and "Painted Lady" in 1908, both marbled types. In 1911 T. H. Chivers of Amesbury, Massachusetts, collected a large number of Japanese iris cultivars, many from Japan. In 1921 his nursery was bought by J. H. Alexander, and subsequently the collection was taken over by Howard E. Weed and his son Thurlow, nurserymen and landscapers, of Beaverton, Oregon, who imported and hybridized and did a great deal to popularize Japanese irises through their writing.

The name "Hobbs" as the source for some of Hallock's stock and for two varieties used by Arlie Payne appears in a number of articles, but unfortunately without further identification. Almost certainly, however, this was the important firm of C. M. Hobbs and Sons, of Bridgeport, Indiana, which assumed that name in 1907 but had been a large supplier of trees and plants since before 1875. Other commercial gardens of the early decades of this century included Wayside Gardens, then of Mentor, Ohio, Robert Wyman of Framingham, Massachusetts, and O. M. Pudor of Puyallup, Washington. Tip Top Nurseries owned by M. F. Stuntz of Williamsville, New York, had a large number of Japanese irises. J. A. Kemp of Little Silver, New Jersey, introduced thirteen Japanese iris seedlings in 1927 and 1928, as well as one named "Achievement," which they listed as an interspecies cross from the *I. ensata* "Harmony" by the *I. laevigata albopurpurea*. If correct this would long antedate the work of Tomino and of Yabuya mentioned in chapter 9 but it must be suspect, since those later efforts suggest that this cross is successful only when *I. laevigata* is the pod parent. Fairmont Gardens of Elizabeth J. Nesmith of Lowell, Massachusetts, also introduced Japanese irises prior to World War II. Hoodacres Gardens of C. F. Barber in Oregon had a very large number of Japanese irises—they registered at least seventy—including those varieties originally grown by Chivers that had reached Oregon through the Weeds.

All of these early efforts leading to the introduction and spread of Japanese irises in this country were carried out by commercial growers and dedicated amateurs. In 1924 their ranks were joined by George M. Reed who, with a Ph.D. in botany, was probably the first scientifically trained botanist to take up the cause of Japanese irises in the United States. His interest began when he was working at the Brooklyn Botanic Garden (Ouweneel 1969b). In 1929 C. Stewart Gager, in his annual report as Director of the Garden, wrote "In April 1920, the Botanic Garden entered into a co-operative agreement with American Iris Society to maintain here a test garden for beardless irises and to make a special study of their culture, breeding, diseases, classification, nomenclature and comparative merit. . . . In 1924 Dr. Reed, Curator of Plant Pathology, took charge of the project" (Ouweneel 1969b, 13). In 1924 and 1925 Reed assembled a collection of these irises from various sources for planting at the Botanic Garden and developed a detailed protocol for the studies to be undertaken. By 1926 a progress report noted that Japanese irises had been received from eight American growers and one in Great Britain. Eighty-two varieties had been received from John Lewis Childs, Inc., of Flowerfield, Long Island, including "practically all of the varieties originated as seedlings by that firm and many of the earlier introductions of Hallock" (Ouweneel 1969b, 14). By 1929 it was concluded that the project had "reached a stage where a trip to Japan was essential for the purpose of making first-hand studies of the history, culture, breeding, nomenclature, etc. of Japanese varieties" (Ouweneel 1969b, 17). The American Iris Society helped the Botanic Garden to finance that trip. Reed remained in Japan from March through July 1930 visiting nurseries and gardens. One important result of this visit was his help in establishing there a society concerned with Japanese irises. The planting at the Brooklyn Botanic Garden grew until in 1939 it included approximately 350 varieties of Japanese irises as well as other beardless types. In 1935 the Farmingdale Iris Garden had been established cooperatively on Long Island by the Brooklyn Botanic Garden and the New York State Institute of Applied Agriculture. Japanese irises were planted there as a landscape project and did well according to Reed's report: "In contrast to the behavior of the Tall Bearded iris, the Japanese, Siberian and miscellaneous species have given very fine results" (Ouweneel 1969b, 18). Some 150 varieties from Farmingdale were taken in pots for a display planting at the 1940 World's Fair. Dr. Reed retired in 1946 and moved to Pittsburgh, where a planting of Japanese irises was established at the Phipps Conservatory of the City of Pittsburgh, but all were stolen or lost. Dr. Reed died in 1956. Unfortunately the gardens of Japanese irises he helped to establish at the Brooklyn Botanic Garden, Farmingdale, and Pittsburgh have all disappeared.

The long-term results have been happier at other pioneering public gardens. One of these began in 1927 when Hamilton Carr Bland purchased a pond in Sumter, South Carolina, and created the Swan Lake Iris Gardens, which are now famous for their display of Japanese irises and their week-long festival at bloom time, usually beginning about May 10. The park was expanded through the generosity of A. T. Heath and now consists of 168 acres and draws over one hundred thousand people during the festival.

Incontestably, the modern period in the United States began with W. Arlie Payne of Terre Haute, Indiana. Payne purchased his first tall bearded irises in 1910. This acquisition started a hobby that by 1919 had grown to commercial proportions, which he combined with his professions of nurseryman and landscape architect. In 1925, with his interest stimulated by a catalog of the Hobbs Nursery, Arlie Payne ordered his first four Japanese irises including "Mahogany" and "Uchu." His interest grew and in 1928 he bought ten more from Childs. That same year Franklin B. Mead of Fort Wayne, Indiana, a director of the American Iris Society, imported twenty varieties from Japan. Following Mead's advice, Payne obtained six Japanese imports. He had already started breeding irises, and now, working with the imported Edos, he developed his own varieties which were critically tested, and only those seedlings that proved to be improvements in form, color, pattern, substance, or branching were introduced to the public. Unlike his predecessors, Payne kept meticulous records of his crosses and made his charts available to anyone interested. The magnitude of his effort is illustrated by the fact that at one time his garden contained some eleven thousand plants and his seedlings totaled in all more than one hundred thousand. A few Higos entered his breeding pool in the later years but the Payne cultivars are essentially of Edo origin.

Payne was active in the affairs of the American Iris Society, which presented him with the coveted Hybridizers' Medal in 1965. The most outstanding hybridizer of Japanese irises this country has produced, he did more than any other person to establish their importance. Over a period of forty years he introduced 170 varieties. One of his greatest achievements was "Immaculate Glitter," introduced in 1963, a dark red-violet double with a distinctive white edge. Three of his introductions received awards at the Japanese iris display of the International Garden Exposition in Germany in 1963. "Blue Nocturne" received a gold medal, "Fashion Model" a silver, and "Orchid Majesty" a bronze. He twice received the Payne Award, the highest honor a Japanese iris can win, for "Strut and Flourish" in 1966 and for "Dancing Waves" in 1968.

Walter and Louise Marx of Boring, Oregon, became interested in all types of irises as a hobby in the 1930s. In 1937 Walter Marx ordered a collection of Japanese irises from Japan and began his wonderfully successful work with them. He soon became convinced that the Higo varieties were the best for his purposes and his hybridizing program was based on them. He therefore called his seedlings his Marhigo strain. The first Marhigo appeared in his catalog in 1953 and between then and the late 1960s some one hundred were offered for sale. The beautiful pictures in full color in the catalogs of the Walter Marx Nursery in the 1950s and 1960s probably did more to popularize Japanese irises than any other single factor. Among the most popular Marx varieties are "Blue Lagoon," "Frilled Enchantment," "Frosted Pyramid," "Gay Gallant," "Snowy Hills," "Summer Storm," "World's Delight," "Flashing Koi," "Good Omen," "Sorcerer's Triumph," "Peacock's Dance," "Persian Rug," "Reign of Glory," and "Rose Prelude." These and many others are grown and greatly admired in gardens throughout the United States and other countries. Louise Marx was also a hybridizer and some of the many irises introduced by the nursery bear her name.

By the early 1970s ill health and other circumstances had interfered with the garden and the hybridizing program. Fortunately, Alan and Dorothy Rogers who lived nearby in Sherwood, Oregon, had become friends of Walter and Louise Marx and began to learn from them. After the death of Walter Marx in 1978 the Rogers, as well as some other growers, took over the Marhigos from Louise Marx, and hence this important breeding line continues. Indeed, the Rogers continue to select and introduce outstanding seedlings from crosses made by Walter Marx. Between 1983 and 1988 they introduced ten Marx seedlings in this way and Melrose Gardens of Stocketon, California, has introduced four others.

In 1946 C. A. Swearengen moved to Terra Haute near Arlie Payne and was at once attracted by the beauty of the Japanese irises. The two became friends and under the tutelage of Payne, Swearengen began his own breeding program starting with twenty Payne seedlings and subsequently adding Marhigos to his breeding stock. He introduced twenty Japanese irises including "Blue Honey," "Mulberry Pie," "Oriental Harmony," and "Vestal Trident." He was the first president of the Society for Japanese Iris and did much to increase interest in these flowers.

Fred Maddocks of Fair Oaks, California, was another American pioneer who became interested in Japanese irises about 1940 and began breeding his own strain from a starter collection of imports and some of the early Marhigos. His lovely mallow pink "Leave Me Sighing" won the second Payne Award in 1967, and "Hue and Cry" also won this award in 1973. Among his other admired introductions are "Banners on Parade," "Evening Episode," "Extravagant Plumes," "Geisha Gown," "Geisha Parasol," "Geisha Mischief," "Time and Tide," and "Evening Reverie."

Jonnye Rich of Roseville, California, is another hybridizer of particular importance from this period. She ordered her first irises from Marx in 1955 and started her breeding program with two chance pods from those flowers. Subsequently, she was helped with advice and seedlings by Fred Maddocks. By 1988 she had introduced eleven cultivars including "Center of Attention," "Enchanting Melody," and "Frostbound." Her "Star at Midnight" received the Payne Award in 1969 and "Tuptim," another universal favorite, in 1978. All of Jonnye Rich's plants as well as those of Maddocks, Violet Worley, and Thorton Abel, and some of Marx and of Shuichi Hirao have been introduced by Melrose Gardens of Stocketon, California, which, especially through the interest of Ben R. Hager, has played a very significant role in spreading the popularity of Japanese and other irises both by introducing the hybrids of others and by Hager's own hybridizing achievements.

Another hybridizer of the years following World War II was Arthur H. Hazzard of Kalamazoo, Michigan. He was keenly interested in gardening all his life and first started with bearded irises in the early 1920s. He was "on friendly terms with Japanese irises since around 1926" (Welch 1983) but it was not until 1957 that they became a primary interest. At that time he started crossing the seven varieties he had, all of them dating from 1926 or earlier. In 1958 he first visited Arlie Payne and began adding some Payne varieties and some Marhigos to his breeding stock. He introduced his first Japanese iris in 1963 and introduced eighty-seven in all. He first won the Payne Award in 1971 for "Numazu," followed by "Prairie Love Song" in 1975 and "Prairie Velvet" in 1979. Among his other excellent cultivars are "Prairie Glory," "Prairie Indigo," "Prairie Fantasy," "Prairie Delight," the extremely prolific "Prairie Frost," "Prairie Chief," and "Prairie Noble." Hazzard served the interest of Japanese irises in many ways. Through his influence the first accredited exhibition of Japanese irises in the United States was held in Kalamazoo in 1963 under the sponsorship of the Southwestern Michigan Iris Society, and he played an active part from 1961 to 1963 in the formation of the Society for Japanese Irises. It was his example and encouragement that attracted others in the local area to become growers and hybridizers and made Kalamazoo a center for Japanese iris culture in the United States.

Since the days of these early breeders, interest in Japanese irises in the United States has increased steadily, and there are now many serious hybridizers who have already introduced lovely, improved cultivars and whose efforts assure many more to come. A list of these hybridizers is given in Appendix D.

Once before, in the early decades of this century, Japanese irises enjoyed a period of great popularity in the United States, which then declined. This decline was surely due to lack of understanding of their basic cultural requirements leading to losses and the impression that they were difficult to grow. With the modern widespread knowledge of those requirements goes the understanding that if their needs are met they are, indeed, among the easiest flowers to grow successfully. Coupled with their other lovely qualities this gives promise of a bright future with continued enjoyment of the magnificent cultivars of today and a progression of beautiful new ones.

The history and organization of the Society for Japanese Irises are discussed in appendix A.

CHAPTER 3　※　*Classification*

As noted at the beginning of this book, Japanese iris is the common name for the lovely flowers known in Japan as *hanashōbu*.* Their correct botanical name is *Iris ensata,* a species in series *Laevigatae* of the beardless (Apogon) irises. In the earlier decades of this century there was some speculation that *I. ensata* and *I. laevigata* might be the same (Ouweneel 1968, 1969a; Davidson 1980) and also speculation that modern Japanese irises might be hybrids resulting from natural crosses of those two wild species. These questions have long since been settled and it is now fully accepted that modern Japanese irises are derived from *I. ensata* alone with no admixture of any other species (Kuribayashi and Hirao 1971, Westmeyer 1978, Davidson 1980).

For many years the botanical name used for Japanese irises in the western world was *Iris kaempferi,* the name given to them by von Siebold in 1886 (Ouweneel 1968). That designation was discovered to be taxonomically incorrect because what was clearly the same species had been already named *Iris ensata* in 1794 by Thunberg. In recent years the correct name has come more and more into use, and in 1985 the Society for Japanese Irises took an official stand on the issue, adopting the name *Iris ensata* for its use. Because the incorrect botanical name was widely used for so many years, the name *I. kaempferi* was added parenthetically: "*Iris ensata* (formerly kaempferi)," as an interim compromise until the correct term should be sufficiently well known to make clarification unnecessary.

This story is an excellent example of the confusion that can be caused by taxonomic errors. In this instance, indeed, the confusion

*Japanese and Latinized botanical names are explained in the glossary.

goes even farther because for many years the name *Iris ensata* had been erroneously given to an iris of series *Ensata*. The correction in the use of *I. ensata* for Japanese irises made necessary the correction of the name of the other species. At first it was determined that this species had earlier been described under the name *I. biglumis* but subsequently it was discovered that it had been still earlier described under the name *I. lactea*, requiring a second change in its name.

One other possibility of error must be mentioned. The term Japanese irises used in common garden parlance must not be confused with *Iris japonica*, which is the botanical name of an entirely distinct group of irises belonging in series *Evansia*.

In the classification of the genus *Iris* by Lawrence (1953), which is used by the American Iris Society, Japanese irises are placed in series *Laevigatae* together with *I. laevigata*, *I. pseudacorus*, *I. versicolor*, and *I. virginica*.

Classification within the group of Japanese irises can be made in several ways. In Japan, as explained in chapter 1 they have been classified as Edo, Higo, or Ise types in accordance with the geographic area with which they were identified (Kuribayashi and Hirao 1971, Westmeyer 1978, Miller and Bauer 1987).

The Edo irises are of single (three falls—downward arching or flaring segments), double (six falls), and multipetaled types. Over the hundreds of years of their development they have evolved in a variety of forms and colors. In general the flower form is simpler than those of the Higo and Ise irises. The standards and falls are of only moderate width and do not overlap at the hafts, and by the second day in varieties in which the hafts lengthen there may be small spaces between the falls at the center of double and multipetaled flowers. The flower stalks are taller than the leaves and are often branched. Even in the early period they were bred mainly for garden use rather than pot culture. In those of single form, standards are relatively large, although small in comparison with the standards of tall bearded irises. The styles are small and held in a somewhat flat position. Style tips are simple and round without the tufting often seen in Higo and Ise flowers. The Edo type is illustrated in figure 1 and in plate 5.

Higo varieties, which were developed from Edos starting in the 1860s, also carry their flowers well above the leaves, but in contrast to the Edos, they were developed for pot culture. In order to allow all the energy of the plant to go into the production of one magnificent bloom any branches were removed early as was the second bud at the terminal. Hence, there was no incentive to breed for improved branching. In recent years, however, Higos have also been bred for garden use, and effort has been directed to branching. Higos are of single, double, and multipetaled forms. They have the largest flowers, up to 12 inches or even more in diameter. Falls are wide and overlapping and often nicely ruffled. The styles tend to be large and are held at about 45 degrees with prominent terminal tufts (petaloids). Examples are shown in figures 2, 3, and 11 and in plate 7.

Ise varieties began to be developed about 1800, although the name Ise was not used until about 1910. They were bred from wild species of *I. ensata,* probably from different areas than those from which the Edos and Higos came. Their stalks are about the same height as the leaves and originally they were of only single type. Like the Higos they were bred for pot culture. Their falls are of pendant form. Colors, which include pink and pale blue, tend to be soft and without sharp contrasts or bold patterns. Plate 6 shows a lovely example of the Ise type.

For many years Higo and Ise breeding lines were kept distinct, but more recently they have been crossed with each other and also with Edos in Japan and other countries, and their distinctive features are now less apparent.

In Japan, irrespective of the number of petals and whether Edo, Higo or Ise, there is another classification, based on whether the flower tends to be essentially the same from the first day to the third or whether it changes from day to day or hour to hour. Hirao refers to these two types as normal flowers and acting flowers (Hirao 1963). The act refers to the unfolding of the bud as it opens and the subsequent changes in the flower. Some cultivars, the normal flowers, do not perform the act whereas others, especially among the Higos and Ises, do. See also page 52.

In the United States, Europe, and Japan, classification is based on features of the flowers. The earliest American classifications merely separated the flowers according to their colors (Reed 1928, Westmeyer 1965) but, although color is, of course, of paramount importance in describing the flowers, it was not very useful as a means of classification, especially as the number of cultivars rapidly increased. Currently, classification is based chiefly on the number of petals occupying the position of falls. Those with three falls and three standards are commonly called three-petaled ones or singles, and those without standards and all six petals in the position of falls are called six-petaled ones or doubles. Flowers with more than six petals (usually nine or twelve) are referred to as multipetaled types. These types are illustrated in figures 1–3 and 5–8. Flowers with multiple petals at the center are sometimes called peony or pompon types.

The practice of calling the single and double flowers three- and six-petaled types has the authority of established usage but is an inaccurate use of terms. In the singles, three petals refers to the falls but botanically the standards are the petals and the falls are sepals (Porter 1959); and if the term petals is used in its common meaning of any blade-like floral part, both singles and doubles have six petals. It would be more correct to call them flowers with three or six falls. The terms single, double, and multipetaled for the three types, although also well established, are not very appropriate either since both singles and doubles have the same number of segments, but at least they do not violate botanical meaning. In this book the terms singles and doubles, or three and six falls will be used. When the word petal occurs it will have the common meaning, not the botanical one. In short descriptions of individual cultivars, the abbreviations 3P and 6P are often used. We suggest that 3F and 6F would be more accurate.

Another convenient way of classification is to use the season of bloom, that is, very early, early, midseason, late, very late, continuing bloomers, repeat bloomers, and rebloomers. Size of flower and height of stalk may also serve as aids in classification as, for example, miniatures with small flowers on short stalks (see plate 3), dwarfs with similarly short stalks but larger flowers, intermediates or small-flowered types (plate 5), and those of usual size, including the very large and very tall ones. Specific measurements, although given in descriptions of individual cultivars, have not yet been established for purposes of classification, as has been done for the median bearded irises. In practice, plants referred to as miniatures have flowers about 4 inches in diameter on stalks 10 to 18 inches tall and those called intermediates have flowers 4 to 5½ inches in diameter on stalks 24 to 30 inches tall.

Since 1979 when the first tetraploid Japanese iris was introduced it has also been necessary to distinguish between diploids and tetraploids in classification.

Tetraploid Japanese Irises

Genes, the genetic determinants for all forms of life, are contained in bodies of microscopic size called chromosomes, situated in the

FIGURE 1. Single flower (three falls) of Edo type. Fairly open form with spaces between the falls. Standards are quite large as in many singles of Edo type. Form is vertically arched and modestly ruffled.

FIGURE 2. Single flower (three falls) of Higo type with wide, overlapping falls and small standards. Form is flaring and modestly ruffled.

FIGURE 3. Double flower (six falls) of Higo type.

nuclei of cells. Every living species has a standard number of chromosomes. In the case of Japanese irises this number is twenty-four, which consists of two sets of twelve, one set from each parent. Since the plant cells contain two sets of chromosomes, they and the plants they make up are called diploids, meaning twofold. For causes that are not known, some plants, over the eons of their existence, have doubled their number of chromosomes naturally, and these are called tetraploids, meaning fourfold. The modern tall bearded irises are an example of tetraploid plants derived from several Mediterranean species that had become tetraploid naturally.

Since tetraploid forms are superior to diploid forms in some respects, botanists have attempted to find means of inducing chromosome doubling. Many physical and chemical measures were tried with little success until the 1930s, when it was discovered that chromosome doubling can be accomplished by the use of the drug colchicine, obtained from the autumn crocus, *Colchicum autumnale,* used in medicine since the days of early Greece (Eigsti and Dustin 1955). Chromosome doubling has not been known to occur naturally in Japanese irises, but it has been brought about by the use of colchicine. The late Max Steiger in Germany used colchicine in 1957 to induce tetraploid Japanese irises (Steiger 1963, 1964) but apparently they were never introduced, and all were lost during his long terminal illness. Orville Fay, who used colchicine in his work with *hemerocallis,* also induced a few tetraploid Japanese irises in the late 1950s, but they were lost, and thereafter he limited his work with colchicine to daylilies. Some tetraploids or partial tetraploids were induced in Japan by Mitsuda in the early 1960s but were not fertile and apparently aroused little interest. The late Shuichi Hirao also attempted to develop tetraploids, starting in 1952, but he had no suitable colchicine. Subsequently, he obtained active colchicine and believed he had partial success but, to our knowledge, his results were not tested, and none were introduced.

Serious interest in the induction of tetraploid Japanese irises began in 1960 when the author, on a visit to Orville Fay, learned the use of colchicine for that purpose and the following spring began to apply it in Siberian and Japanese irises (McEwen 1966, 1971a). Success came fairly quickly in the Siberians but slowly in the Japanese and the first tetraploid, "Raspberry Rimmed," was not introduced until 1979. Progress then was rapid and many tetraploid cultivars are now available. In recent years Eckard Berlin in West Germany has developed a number of tetraploid Japanese irises, as have Jill Copeland and several others in the United States. Interest has revived also in Japan, where work is being undertaken by Mototeru Kamo, Hioshi Shimizu, Tsutomu Yabuya, and others.

When a plant is treated with colchicine there are four possible results: (1) It may be killed outright. (2) It may be unaffected and remain diploid. (3) It may be completely converted to the tetraploid state. (4) It may be only partially converted—a chimera.* In practice the treated plant is rarely fully converted; most of those that survive are unaffected or are chimeras. Depending on the degree of conversion, crossing two chimeras may result in diploid or tetraploid seed-

*Two terms used in discussing tetraploids are polyploid and chimera. The term polyploid refers to plants with any number of chromosomes more than the normal diploid number, that is, chimeras, triploids, tetraploids or those with still higher numbers. Chimera from a mythological Greek monster with the head of a lion, the body of a goat, and the tail of a serpent, has been adopted for plants and animals composed of tissues of different types, for instance part diploid and part polyploid. Chimeras may be subdivided into periclinal and sectorial. In periclinal chimeras some of the pollen grains and ovules of every flower are diploid and some polyploid. In sectorial chimeras one complete section of the plant is diploid and the other polyploid.

lings. A chimera may, in time, revert to the diploid state but once the second generation of tetraploidy is reached the plant is completely stabilized and can no longer revert.

It should be noted that tetraploids are not mutants in the modern sense since there is no change in the chemical nature of the genetic material (DNA) of the genes, merely twice as much of it.

Features of Tetraploids

Features of tetraploid cultivars are similar to those of diploids, with exaggeration of some characteristics. Leaves and stalks are stouter but not taller and are of a deeper green color. Flowers are larger and of flaring form with petals of very strong substance. Plate 4 shows a sectorial chimera illustrating the diploid and tetraploid forms of the same cultivar. Colors are similar, since the pigments are the same, but usually they are richer because each cell contains approximately twice as much pigment. Such features as ruffling and velvety texture tend to be increased. From the standpoint of the hybridizer, the greater number of chromosomes and hence of genes enhances the potential for the development of new traits and features, and tetraploids have been essential in the creation of fertile interspecies hybrids. After five hundred years of diploid crosses it is probable that much of the potential of those efforts has been achieved. The advent of tetraploids introduces a challenging new departure.

Methods for the induction of tetraploidy are discussed in appendix E.

CHAPTER 4   ❋   *Characteristics*

The Wild Species I. ensata

THE PLANTS AND FLOWERS of the species *I. ensata* are similar in various parts of Japan, China, Siberia, Manchuria, and other places where they grow in the wild (see figure 4 and plates 1 and 2). Foliage is upright and about 25 to 40 inches in height and ½ inch in width. The bloom stalks are usually 3 to 10 inches taller than the leaves. Flowers are of the single (three falls) type, although rare ones with an odd number of segments occur, and are approximately 4½ inches in diameter. Falls and standards are rather narrow and the falls are pendant. Branching is not constant. Two buds are held at the terminal with one more on a branch. Color is shades of reddish purple with yellow signals, and a few have very light styles. White and pinkish forms occur in the wild but are not common, although there may have been more a century or two ago.

Botanically, the term *Iris ensata* Thunberg var. *spontanea* has been used for the species and *Iris ensata* Thunberg var. *ensata* for the thousands of cultivated seedlings that have come from the species (Tomino 1968). In common garden usage the former are usually called the wild species and the latter the modern hybrids or, in Japan, Japanese garden irises.

Features of Modern Hybrids

In view of the similarity of the wild species throughout Japan, the striking variation in the hybrids that have been developed from them is remarkable and suggests that mutations may have played an important role in their development. The various characteristics of the mod-

FIGURE 4. Example of the wild *Iris ensata* species with spaces between the pendent, rather narrow falls, and tailored form.

ern hybrids are discussed in the following paragraphs. At the outset it must be emphasized that the characteristics discussed, especially size of flowers and height, are greatly affected by the conditions under which the plants are grown.

Types

Of the three principal types of Japanese irises—singles, doubles, and multipetaled—the single type may be thought of as the basic one since it is the form of the wild species. In it the various primary structures are present in sets of three: three falls, three standards, three styles with their stigmas, three stamens with their anthers. Most deviations from that basic form occur when one structure replaces another or so closely mimics another that it cannot be readily distinguished from it. In the normal double flower the three standards mimic falls, producing a flower with six falls and no standards. In multipetaled flowers this mimicry extends to the stamens and/or styles producing flowers with nine or twelve or more petals.

Flowers of multipetaled type differ not only in the number of petals but also in the character of the extra petals and of the flowers. In some the extra segments are merely petaloids, as in figure 5. In some with fully formed though small extra petals, the flower is neatly organized (figures 6 and 7) but in most the form is quite informal (figure 8) and in some the total appearance is so lacking in organization that the character of the flower is lost.

Only rarely does a flower occur in which more than three of any primary structure is present without a corresponding reduction in the number of one of the other primary structures (Ackerman and Williams 1982). An example of one such cultivar is "Gosen-no-Takara," with flowers having three, four, and five falls on a single plant.

Form

In each type the form may be pendant with the falls hanging down in pendent or vertically arched fashion (figures 1 and 4, plate 6), horizontally flaring in disk-like fashion (figures 2 and 10, plate 7), or anywhere in between the two. Falls may be narrow with spaces between (figure 4 and plate 5) or wide and overlapping (figure 2 and plates 7, 17). In the single flowers the standards range from very small to medium sized but are never as large as those of tall bearded irises. In some double cultivars the three falls of the inner group corresponding to the standards of the single flowers may remain partly upright the first day and not give the flowers the normal appearance of a double until the second day. Those irises with multiple petals tend to have a round, full form. In flowers of all types the segments may be smooth (tailored), as in figures 4 and 9 and plates 2, 5, and 7, or ruffled as in figure 11 and plates 8, 13, and 19. The edges may be modestly crimped, but so far lacing like that in some bearded irises has not appeared. In Japan some unusual flowers, for instance "Gyokuhoren," do not unfold their falls and remain in somewhat globu-

FIGURE 5. Example of the multipetaled flower in which the "extra" segments are merely petaloids derived from the stamens.

FIGURE 6. Multipetaled flower with nine nicely formed petals.

FIGURE 7. Multipetaled flower with thirteen petals in which the extra petals are derived from both stamens and styles. Nicely organized, compact form.

FIGURE 8. Multipetaled flower ("Frosted Pyramid") with nine or ten petals. Character is informal in an attractive way.

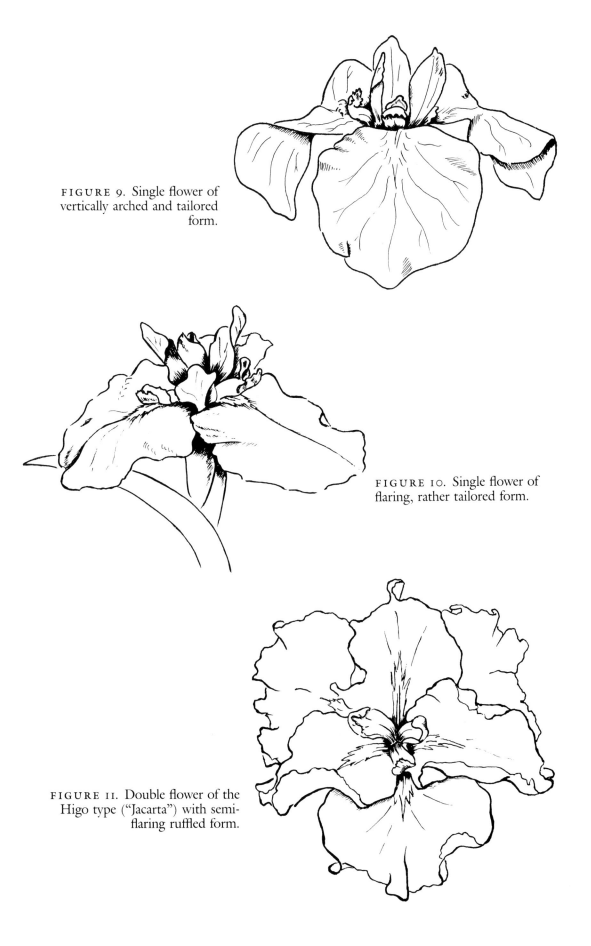

FIGURE 9. Single flower of vertically arched and tailored form.

FIGURE 10. Single flower of flaring, rather tailored form.

FIGURE 11. Double flower of the Higo type ("Jacarta") with semi-flaring ruffled form.

lar form, or do not open the falls fully, so that the flower forms a cup.

Size

Most Japanese iris flowers are from 5 to 9 inches in diameter on stalks from 26 to 40 inches tall. Some very large ones may reach 10 to 12 inches in diameter and stalks may also be taller. At the other extreme are the charming miniatures with 4-inch flowers on 10- to 18-inch stalks (plate 3). In many flowers the falls tend to increase somewhat in size throughout the life of the flower.

Colors, Signals, and Patterns

The range of colors of Japanese irises is less than in the tall beardeds but this is offset by the great variety of patterns and color combinations, many of which are extremely striking.

The colors of modern cultivars include shades of violet-blue and purple from very light to dark, wine red and lavender-pink of varying intensity, and white, which is well represented in shades from glistening white to pale cream (plates 7 and 8). There are many purples from both the blue and the red side but no flowers of spectrum blue or red as yet, although progress toward those goals is being made (plates 9, 10, 11, and 12). True pink has nearly been attained (plate 13). There are as yet no yellow Japanese irises, and hybridizing efforts to extend the yellow of the signals out onto the falls have failed. A few of the creamy yellow cultivars have a yellowish tint (plate 8) but true yellow exists only in hybrids from crosses of *I. pseudacorus* by Japanese irises (plate 14). The color of many cultivars may become lighter from the first to third day but not unattractively, and this is a normal feature.

A most distinctive feature of Japanese irises is the signal at the base of each fall in the single flowers and of all six falls in the doubles. The usual color of the signals ranges from light yellow to very rich yellow approaching orange. Signals of yellow tinged with green are not uncommon, and some of distinct green are beginning to appear (plate 15). Some flowers are self-colored, with no visible signals (plate 7).

One of the most striking features of Japanese irises is their wide range of color patterns. Flowers of solid colors, so-called selfs, form the basic background of any garden, but in a planting of Japanese irises the overall effect is dramatized by flowers with distinct patterns of the following sorts:

Veined: very fine dark lines follow the anatomical "veins" against the white or pale background of the falls (plate 16).

Lined: white lines, also referred to as rays, follow the anatomical veins against dark falls; the lines, which are wider than the veins, may be quite wide and striking and often are branched, especially at their outer ends. They are best when sharply outlined. The lines usually start at white areas surrounding the signals (plate 17).

Sanded: falls and often the standards too in single flowers are covered with extremely small darker dots and very short broken lines against a lighter background usually of rather soft colors, giving the impression of scattered sand (plate 18).

Brushed: basically similar to the sanded pattern, this refers to dots so minute that the appearance is that of a brushing or wash of somewhat darker color over a lighter one (plate 19).

Edged: a narrow dark edging surrounds light falls and standards, or a very light edging surrounds darker petals. The edging may be merely a fine line or as much as ⅛ inch in width (plates 20 and 21).

Rimmed: wide, dark rims, often with irregular inner margins, surround white or very light central areas (plate 22). In some flowers this pattern is reversed with the rim lighter than the central area (plate 18).

Splashed or marbled: a pattern of broken lines, large dots and small irregular patches is formed, usually of light color on dark background (plate 23).

Bitone: flowers of a single color (except for the signals) have standards and/or styles of lighter or darker tone than the falls (plate 24).

Bicolors: most Japanese iris flowers show two colors, the basic one and the yellow or green of the signals, and in some red flowers there are blue tones around the signal. The term bicolor is commonly used, however, only for flowers with a striking contrast between white and a dark color as seen in plate 25. Veined, lined, edged, and rimmed flowers also show two contrasting colors but they are customarily categorized in terms of their distinctive patterns.

Halo: a narrow band of a color that sharply contrasts with that of the falls surrounds the signal. This is most clearly shown in flowers with dark halos against light colored falls (plate 26). Halos are seen also as white bands around the signals of dark falls but these are less easy to categorize because often the white areas are too large to be so designated and become the pale central areas seen in many dark flowers from which, in many cases, white lines radiate out toward the edges of the falls.

Time and Duration of Bloom

Time of bloom differs greatly, of course, from southern to northern regions. In general one may say that Japanese irises start to bloom about a month after tall bearded irises. Since the average period of bloom is two to three weeks, most garden plantings show bloom for a month or less. However, if very early, mid-season, and very late cultivars are included in the same planting, the period of bloom can easily be increased to six weeks or more (Ackerman and Williams 1981). Under particular environmental conditions the period of bloom may alter. In Del Mar, California, for example, bloom can occur off and on over a six-month period, but the flowers tend to be smaller and stalks shorter (Gunther 1987). Preliminary experience in a new planting in central Florida suggests that there may be a somewhat similar spread of bloom dates there, with some starting in March and peak bloom in May extending into June, and with considerable repeat bloom as well as robust growth and outstanding branching and bud count (Padgett 1987, 1988).

Some cultivars have the extremely desirable ability to bloom, individually, for weeks longer than the average. Some, which are appropriately called continuing bloomers, do so by sending up successive bloom stalks for five weeks or more. Other varieties prolong the duration of bloom by having a second bloom period. It must be emphasized that this second bloom differs sharply in its timing from that of the rebloom of bearded irises (McEwen 1983, 1986a), which usually occurs following a lapse of two to four months. In Japanese and Siberian irises the second bloom usually comes after a period of only one to three weeks without bloom. To emphasize this difference in timing, it has been recommended that the second period of bloom in these beardless irises be called repeat bloom to distinguish it from the rebloom of the bearded irises. Several of the better repeat bloomers continue to show good bloom for more than nine weeks, with an interval of only a week or two during that time without their handsome flowers. The repeat bloomers can be further categorized as occasional repeaters, in which second bloom usually is meager and does not occur every year; dependable repeaters, which can be expected to have a good period of second bloom yearly if well grown; and preferential repeaters with second bloom superior to the first. In addition to repeat bloomers there are a few cultivars that rebloom in the fall as the bearded rebloomers do, and a very few, such as the one shown in plate 27, that both repeat and rebloom (McEwen 1986b). The performance of all types of remontancy in Japanese irises is greatly affected by the conditions under which they are grown.

As well as the blooming period of the plant, it is also desirable to extend the length of bloom of individual flowers. One of the shortcomings of Japanese irises is the flowers' usual lifespan of only three days under the best conditions and only, perhaps, two in hot, dry regions, but progress is being made in developing cultivars with flowers remaining fresh for four and five days (Ackerman 1973; Ackerman and Williams 1981).

Since all the features that contribute to longer bloom, both of the plant as a whole and of the individual flowers, are largely under genetic control, it can be anticipated that these extremely desirable traits will be enhanced still further through continued selective breeding.

Texture, Substance and Durability

Texture relates to the surface characteristics of the petals. It may be of various types, such as glossy, matte (the opposite of glossy), smooth, creped, satiny, glistening, diamond dusted, or velvety. As these adjectives imply, texture affects the quality of the color. Velvety texture, especially, tends to enhance the richness of color, particularly dark reds and purples (plate 12).

Substance, which relates to the deep tissue characteristics of the petals, may be strong and firm, light and flexible, or weak. Strong substance is seen in flowers of flaring and semi-flaring form. Those of a gracefully downward curving type usually have lighter substance. Weak substance is seen in petals that hang limply.

Durability has in the past been sometimes confused with substance but the two are quite distinct. Durability refers to the ability of the flower to remain fresh a normal number of days and to resist damage by wind, rain, heat, and other adverse conditions. It is of paramount importance. No matter how beautiful a flower may be it is of little value if that beauty fades too quickly or is destroyed by a light rain or heat that is not harmful to others.

Leaves and Bloomstalks

One of the valuable attributes of Japanese irises is the capacity of the leaves to remain strong, upright, green and healthy throughout the spring, summer, and fall, making the plants attractive garden subjects long after the end of bloom. There may be some browning of leaf tips by late summer but usually not in a way that makes them unattractive. An occasional plant has leaves that tend to sprawl throughout the season or after bloom. Such a plant deserves no place in the garden.

A characteristic feature of the leaves that helps distinguish them from those of other irises is the prominent midrib which is visible, and can also be felt running the length of the leaf.

As explained earlier, in Japan, when plants were being grown in pots for display indoors there was no incentive to breed for branching. Even in the early days, however, Edo varieties were grown for garden as well as pot culture and therefore branching was encouraged. In modern times, with interest in Japanese irises chiefly as garden plants, improved branching and bud count have become a major concern of hybridizers, and there are now cultivars with up to three branches plus the terminal and as many as eight or nine buds per stalk.

Branching usually is an asset in ensuring longer bloom but it must be emphasized that this demands that the branches be suitably spaced and formed so that the flowers do not interfere with one another, and the bud count is superior. Since the chief value of branching is to give long bloom, a cultivar with only one branch or with none which continues to send up stalks over a long period can be better than one with multiple mediocre branches.

The rhizomes of Japanese irises are smaller than those of tall bearded irises. A distinctive feature is a reddish tint which can be seen very clearly on the cut surface. The cut surface of *I. pseudacorus* has the same reddish appearance. Roots of Japanese irises may also show spots or streaks of red where an injury has permitted the red pigment to ooze out. The chemical nature of the pigment is not yet known. Preliminary tests indicate that it is not anthocyanin, carotenoid, or quinonoid, and it appears to be an unusual type of pigment (Harborne 1988).

1. Clump of the species *Iris ensata* growing wild in Japan near Sendai, Miyagi Prefecture.

2. A flower of the wild *Iris ensata* cultivar collected on Hokkaido Island.

3. Miniature with 3½ inch flowers on 15 inch stalks. Part of a flower of moderate size is shown at the top for comparison.

4. Sectorial chimera with diploid flower on the left and tetraploid flower of the same plant on the right. The tetraploid is larger, more ruffled and somewhat richer in color.

5. "Eternal Feminine," an intermediate Japanese iris of Edo type with rather open form and green signals.

6. "Miyoshino," Ise type of lovely pink with vertically arched form.

7. "Immaculate White," a pure white single of Higo type with wide overlapping falls and no visible signal.

8. "Hint of Yellow," a nicely ruffled double, creamy white with light yellow styles.

9. "Oriental Royalty," tetraploid, single, reddish-purple with a few white streaks at the base of the falls, white in the edged styles, and no visible signals.

10. "Crepe Paper," a light-blue double flower with somewhat sanded texture.

11. "Midnight Lagoon," a dark-blue double flower.

12. "Midnight Stars," a dark, wine-red, double flower with velvety texture.

13. "Celestial Pink," a ruffled single of true pink and white. The flower is just opening.

14. "Kimboshi," a clear yellow single hybrid from a cross of *Iris pseudacorus* by a Japanese iris.

15. "Go green," a wide, ruffled, single, tetraploid, pure white with green signals.

16. "Caprician Butterfly," a double flower exhibiting the veined pattern.

17. "Hue and Cry," a reddish-purple double with large white halos and white lines or rays.

18. "Shin-Asahinoyuki," exhibiting the sanded pattern and the reversed rimmed pattern.

19. "Cascade Crest," a fine double flower exhibiting the brushed pattern.

20. "Frilled Enchantment," double flowers with ruffled white falls and dark blue-violet edging.

21. "Japanese Pinwheel," a velvety, dark, wine-red, single tetraploid with all segments sharply edged in white.

22. "Blueberry Rimmed," a large single tetraploid with wide blue-violet rims around white central areas of falls.

23. "Wounded Dragon," double flowers illustrating the marbled or splashed pattern.

24. "Capitol Dandy," soft lavender-pink bitoned single flowers.

25. "Popular Acclaim," bicolored single flowers with white falls and contrasting dark blue-violet standards.

26. "Sayo-no-tuki," illustrating nicely outlined dark blue-violet halos surrounding light yellow signals with short, dark lines in the signals and extending from the halos. This is an unusual and lovely example of an *I. pseudacorus* × *I. ensata* hybrid.

27. An example of a repeating and reblooming Japanese iris with excellent branching. Note the well-developed seed pod from earlier bloom and new flowers opening on the repeat/rebloom stalk.

28. A planting of Japanese irises beside the water at Kyoto Heian Shrine Iris Garden.

29. General garden view at Ensata Gardens, Galesburg, Michigan.

30. A small raked-sand type of Japanese garden at Ensata Gardens, Galesburg, Michigan.

31. Large display of Japanese irises at the Tokyo Botanical Garden.

CHAPTER 5　　〜〜〜　*Culture*

THIS CHAPTER is concerned with the planting and culture of mature plants. Planting seeds and young seedlings is discussed in Chapter 11.

Let it be emphasized at the start that the culture of Japanese irises is easy in most temperate zones such as the United States (except for the deep south), Europe, and Japan provided their basic requirements are met, and they can be successfully grown even in environmentally unsuitable regions by the use of special methods.

Basic Culture

The particular requirements of Japanese irises that must be born in mind in preparing a bed for them and in caring for them are the following: (1) they require a somewhat acid soil, (2) they need abundant water, (3) they are heavy feeders, (4) mature divisions are planted with their rhizomes deeper than those of other irises, (5) they usually need to be dug, trimmed of spent rhizomes and roots and replanted every three or four years, and (6) if their two chief enemies, borers and thrips, appear they must be eradicated. With that general statement of needs let us consider the various aspects of culture in greater detail.

Climate

Japanese irises are adaptable to a wide range of climatic conditions so long as their particular needs are met. They are extremely hardy to cold. Both the wild species and modern hybrids are grown in the central regions of the Hokkaido Island of Japan where temperatures reach −30° F, and the species in Siberia grow at temperatures as low as −50° F. There they are, of course, covered with deep snow (Ito 1966; Hirao 1987; Kamo 1989). It must be noted, however, that modern hybrids subjected to rapid freezing followed by a quick thaw, such as those standing in unprotected pots, can be severely injured (Vogt 1988). Plants in beds covered by thick ice for long periods can also be seriously damaged. A contributing factor in this injury may be the inability of oxygen to reach the plants. Japanese irises can also be grown under semitropic conditions, but in hot, dry regions, especially where the soil is alkaline, special methods are necessary.

Site Selection

Except in hot regions, Japanese irises thrive best in full sun, with a minimum of the equivalent of half a day of sun. With less the plants may grow but tend to be leggy with poor bloom. In very hot regions partial shade is advantageous. Planting at the edge of a pond or stream is excellent both because of the abundant moisture and because of the beauty of the flowers against the water and reflected in it. In regions of high winds, a site where the plants will have protection is important, or a wind break can be provided. Because of the harmful effect of lime, care must be taken that the bed is not placed where it can receive the runoff of water from crushed limestone driveways or seepage from basement walls.

Bed Preparation

Japanese irises prefer a heavy loam, probably because of its ability to retain moisture and nutrients. Lighter and sandy soils should be given a generous admixture of heavier soil and compost, well-rotted manure or other organic material and, if very sandy, even some clay. The soil should be acid in reaction, with pH in the mildly acid range. In a study by Swearengen pH levels from 5.5 to 6.5 were quite satisfactory, with best growth occurring at pH 5.8 (Swearengen 1964). Too much calcium, one of the mineral nutrients utilized by plants, is harmful (Marschner 1986), but whether it exerts some harmful effect *per se* or acts merely by increasing the alkalinity of the soil is uncertain. Indeed, it is not fully understood why some plants need acid soil while others prefer alkaline conditions and most grow well in soils of either sort.

Japanese irises will grow and bloom in soil of neutral or even slightly alkaline reaction, but less well, and they will gradually deteriorate (McEwen 1979). By painstaking selective breeding over many years with thousands of seedlings in soil containing lime and with alkaline pH, Max Steiger, in Germany, developed a strain of Japanese irises that grows well under conditions unsuitable for ordinary ones with regard to calcium, pH, and relative dryness (Steiger 1963). These plants, which he referred to as his Care strain (for *Ca*lcium *re*sistant), are unfortunately rarely found today.

If soil tests show that the pH is not low enough, the soil acidity can be increased by working in a pound of soil sulphur or ferrous sulfate per hundred square feet, or two pounds if the pH is very alkaline. Since such treatment takes up to six months to exert its full effect, if soil tests for a proposed bed indicate the need for treatment it should be done well in advance. Under extremely alkaline conditions the creation of an acid bed may be necessary as described later. Usually, however, the application of soil sulfur or ferrous sulfate when the bed is made and the subsequent use of fertilizer of acid type and mulching with acid type materials such as oak leaves will keep the pH in the desired range for the three years before normal replanting is due, and at that time the bed can be retreated or, preferably, the plants can be moved to a newly acidified bed. Rich (1989), however, reports that in her garden in Roseville, California, the effect of the sulfur may last only a year and must be renewed. Care must be taken that the pH is not lowered too much. Aluminum sulfate appears to work very quickly and if used at all it must be with great care. After its use in one Missouri garden the pH was reduced to 4.5 at which level some plants were lost. At still further reduction to 4.0 pH all plants in that bed died or were seriously affected (Delmez 1989). Clearly, it is essential that if pH modifying materials are to be used periodic measurements of the soil pH must be made.

The area selected for the bed should be dug or tilled to a depth of at least 6 to 10 inches. Ideally it is double dug to a depth of 12 to 16 inches with well-rotted manure dug in at the bottom and soil then replaced so the topsoil is at the bottom and the former subsoil, with the addition of compost, thoroughly aged manure, spent straw, peat moss, or other organic material, is above (Coble 1985). If the area was originally covered with turf, this can be killed with glyphosate (Roundup) or other similar herbicide and, after the double digging, put back at the bottom and dug in with manure and soil. A bed prepared in this painstaking way is ideal for such gross feeders as Japanese irises and encourages deep root growth. However they will do very well in far less elaborately prepared beds as long as the pH is correct and they receive adequate water and fertilizer.

Water

In early times the wild *I. ensata* of Japan grew in marshy meadow areas and subsequently, when collected, tended to be planted in the Tokyo area in rice paddies. In later plantings, such as at the Meiji Shrine and other public and private gardens, the modern plants are often seen along the banks of ponds or in pots actually in the water. Hirao (1984) has explained that this is done not because the plants require it but because of the beauty of the flowers reflected in the water. Probably all these reasons have led to the widely held but erroneous impression that Japanese irises are basically water plants and should be grown in water. The fact is that they are quite at home with their roots in water during spring and summer, but they do not need that treatment and grow magnificently in any well-prepared and cared for garden, provided they receive ample water. A raised bed, of course, should not be used unless copious water can be provided. It is estimated by Coble (1985) that in his garden in Michigan one inch of rain is required weekly and if that much is not provided by nature the amount is augmented by the sprinkler. The amount can be readily measured with a rain gauge or any straight-sided jar or can. Drip irrigation is excellent also. In plantings so constructed that the bed is several inches lower than the surrounding ground or has a raised edge around it, the entire garden area can be flooded once a week or as needed, but there must be means of allowing water to drain off in the fall (Wadekamper 1987).

Today, it is generally accepted that Japanese irises should not be allowed to stand in water or ice over winter. Nevertheless there can be no doubt that under certain conditions some cultivars can do so year after year without apparent harm (Fisk 1948; Ouweneel 1977, 1981; Ross 1978). Comparative trials of plants grown in various ways in relation to water are needed to learn more exactly what their requirements and tolerances are. One such trial in North Carolina has been reported by Wood comparing growth of plants standing in a pond the whole year with others planted in the ground around the pond. Those in the pond had 8 to 10 inches of water over them in the winter and 2 to 3 inches in the summer. The winter temperature seldom dropped below 15 to 20° F. Plants in the pond grew but bloomed three or four weeks later than those in the ground around the pond, and the flowers were smaller and increase much less. A mulch was needed to prevent heaving of plants in the ground but there was no evident heaving of those in the pond (Wood 1987a). Additional trials will be of interest but at present it is advisable to follow the general practice and make sure that water does not stand on the crown of the plants after late fall.

Bauer has reported exceptionally good results growing the plants under boglike conditions, creating artificial bogs by lining excavated beds with plastic sheeting and refilling with topsoil enriched with perlite, sphagnum moss, and manure. The plants do not stand in water, but because of the plastic sheeting, the soil is distinctly moist. The plants in the artificial bogs grew 6 to 12 inches taller than the same cultivars in the ordinary garden beds, made larger clumps, and had many more bloomstalks (Bauer 1989). Padgett found that Japanese irises grown under similar boglike conditions made excellent growth and bloom even in the usually adverse conditions found in central Florida (Padgett, 1987, 1988).

Another excellent way to provide ample water is through the use of soaker-type hose buried 3 to 6 inches deep along the rows. Such beds, well mulched to retain moisture and with the water left on for one or two hours daily, also provide semiboglike conditions. In the author's garden Japanese irises grown in this way have flourished.

Fertilizer

Japanese irises are heavy feeders requiring abundant fertilizer. Except for the preparation of the planting area with well-rotted manure and compost as discussed above, it is generally recommended that newly set plants should not be given fertilizer for about three weeks while they are becoming established. They can then be given a watering of soluble fertilizer for quick effect and granular fertilizer for sustained action. Established plants receive a side dressing of granular fertilizer, with or without the soluble fertilizer, in the spring when the leaves are about 3 inches tall and again following the end of bloom. Watering with soluble fertilizer three or four weeks before expected bloom date is useful, as is a fall dressing with well-rotted manure, which can be tilled into the soil between the rows in the spring or left as part of a spring mulch.

The formulas of granular fertilizers preferred by different growers vary considerably. Kamo (1989) reports that in Japan nitrogen is usually deficient and recommends a formula of 26–10–10. (These figures represent the percentages respectively of nitrogen, phosphorous, and potassium.) Experienced growers in the United States use formulas ranging from the common 5–10–5 to 20–20–20. The irises appear to do well with all. Unquestionably the best course is to have the soil in the particular garden tested and use a formula and amount in accordance with the test results. In the United States it is possible to have a reliable chemical analysis of the soil made by the local Department of Agriculture Extension Service.

Unless the natural pH of the garden soil is 5.8 or below, fertilizer of acid type should be selected. Some growers prefer to use fertilizer of soluble type as a spray, usually the type that makes use of the garden hose, but the soluble fertilizers persist in the soil only about three weeks and, hence, many time-consuming and expensive applications are needed. Most growers use the soluble fertilizers only for occasional booster effect to supplement the granular fertilizer applied in the spring and after bloom.

Mulches

Mulches in the Japanese iris garden are very useful in a number of ways: (1) they provide winter protection, (2) they help control weeds, and (3) they conserve water in the soil. Materials for mulches may be of many sorts, from black plastic sheeting or other synthetic products to organic types such as leaves, oat straw, or wood chips. Hay should be avoided, as it is full of seeds which produce a perennial crop of weeds. Wheat and rye straw also drop seeds which produce winter-hardy perennial seedlings. Oat seedlings are killed by winter cold in regions where the temperature drops to 20°F or lower and hence create no problem the following spring. Seaweed, often used in coastal gardens for some perennials, is not suitable for Japanese irises as it causes alkalinity (McEwen 1988).

If any of the organic mulch materials such as oat straw are unattractive to the grower because of their yellow color, a spray of a solution of ferrous sulphate, one cup to a gallon of water, will darken it quickly to a rusty gray.

For purposes of weed control and water conservation a black plastic sheeting type of mulch is just as good as, or perhaps even more efficient than, an organic mulch, although it is of no value for winter protection and must be discarded when it is too torn for further use, while an organic mulch can be dug in and contribute to the quality of the soil. If used in windy places the edges of the plastic sheets must be buried or firmly held down by other means or they become badly torn. With careful use they may last more than one season before they must be discarded. Some of the newer types now available may last even longer. If plastic sheeting is used on flat garden areas some water is lost to the plants, but some newer types of sheeting permit the water to go through.

Winter Protection: Well-established plants are very winter hardy and if healthy and growing well do not need winter protection except, perhaps, in the coldest regions where they are grown. However, plants that are not in good condition from drought, disease, or having been left too long without replanting, may require a winter mulch to survive in cold regions. Small seedlings with roots still not fully grown and plants of any size moved in the fall too late for root growth to anchor them securely need a mulch to prevent heaving out of the ground during freezes and thaws. The thickness of the mulch needed depends, of course, on the degree of cold. In a Maine garden where temperatures do not often go lower than − 15° F a 10-inch mulch of oat straw is put over the plants needing it after their leaves have turned brown and been cut off. Prior to application of the mulch the area around the plant should be cleaned as thoroughly as possible to remove remnants of cut leaves or other debris that might harbor pests or agents of disease. In the spring the mulch can be spread in the paths between the rows to serve in the other ways in which mulches are useful. After a year or so when this organic mulching material is beginning to rot it can be tilled or dug in to improve the soil.

Control of Weeds: Whether or not a mulch is needed for winter protection it serves admirably in helping to control weeds. Not only is the number of weeds much less in a mulched garden but those that do start are easily removed. Usually this requires hand weeding, because the mulch makes tool cultivating difficult, and tilling turns the mulch into the soil. For weed control an organic mulch of 3-inch thickness usually is sufficient. In areas with alkaline soil an acid-producing mulch such as oak leaves helps maintain soil acidity. Although the hand pulling of weeds that come through the mulch is easy, often requiring no digging, it can be tedious in very large plantings. In such situations Aitken (1987) recommends the use of glyphosate applied with great care on windless days to avoid getting it on the irises.

As well as by mulches weeds may also be controlled by pre-emergent weed-killers such as Simezine and Treflan. All reports agree that these are effective in controlling weeds but caution has been urged because of apparent damage to irises. For Japanese irises, this may occur at once (Warburton 1988) or may be seen as gradual deterioration after several years. If weed-killers are tried it is advisable to use them first on a small section of the garden for at least three years to observe the effect before application to the entire planting.

Water Conservation: A mulch is of special value in the case of plants like Japanese irises which demand much water. Scientific studies have shown that the water content of unmulched soil fluctuates greatly, with peaks of high moisture after rain storms and relative dryness between storms. In contrast the water content of suitably watered soil covered by a mulch remains at a fairly constant level of adequate moisture throughout the year.

Planting

Planting of Japanese irises is in general similar to that of other perennials. A hole of ample diameter and about 16 inches deep is dug and well-rotted or commercial dried cow manure dug in at the bottom. This is then covered with top soil which is used also to form a mound of such height that when the plant is placed on it the crown will be about 1½ to 2 inches below the level of the soil after planting. The roots can then be spread down on the sides of the mound and the soil replaced and thoroughly watered. Placing the plant on a mound and watering ensures that the soil is well distributed around the roots and that there is no air pocket under the plant. It is rather generally accepted that fertilizer, other than the manure used in the preparation of the hole, should not be used until three weeks or so after the planting, when it is scratched in as a side dressing, but some growers use a half strength "starting solution" of acid-type soluble fertilizer instead of water at the time of planting to settle the plants in.

Plants moved from one place in the garden to another should be thoroughly watered the day before transplanting to make sure the roots are moist. Unless the plant is small the soil should be washed off and all spent or damaged roots and rhizomes cut out. The leaves also should be cut back about half their length to help balance the loss of some roots. In the case of plants shipped from a distant place the roots should be examined to be sure they are moist. If any poor roots were left untrimmed by the shipper they should be removed. Any knowledgeable shipper will pack Japanese iris plants so that they arrive with moist roots. Nevertheless it is well to soak the roots in clean water for a few hours before planting.

It is best to leave at least 2 feet between plants, but if space is a critical consideration 18 inches is sufficient. Japanese irises require a planting depth quite different from that of most other irises. The tops of the rhizomes should be 1½ to two inches below the soil surface, since the new roots each year tend to form above the level of the old roots. Unless the rhizomes are deeply planted the new roots tend to be too close to the surface of the soil in three or four years. Indeed, superficially planted Japanese irises may have so few strong, viable roots after a few years that they can be pulled out of the ground without digging. Naturally, such plants cannot stand drought, cold, or other stresses and in areas where the ground freezes they will inevitably be heaved out during freezes and thaws. Even when planted two inches deep most Japanese irises grown in an ordinary garden bed should be lifted, trimmed of dead and unhealthy rhizomes and roots, and replanted every three or four years. Unless this is done they gradually deteriorate. The frequency of replanting can be lessened by planting between ridges or in scooped out depressions several inches deep with the tops of the rhizomes one to two inches below the bottom of the depression (Vogt 1988). The depression serves to hold water and also helps maintain healthy roots, since soil tends gradually to raise the level in the depression and the new roots remain a suitable depth below the surface. Not all the factors which lead to deterioration of plants left too long without transplanting are known. Japanese irises growing beside ponds with their roots constantly in naturally moist soil grow beautifully for many years without being moved, and presumably plants of the species *I. ensata* growing in the wild live for years without transplanting. Nevertheless, hard experience teaches that in the average garden most Japanese irises need to be dug, divided, trimmed of spent roots and rhizomes, and replanted every three or four years. If they are growing well and are firmly in the ground they may be left longer but should be observed carefully from year to year for signs of deterioration.

Time of Planting

Planting of young seedlings must, of course, be done in spring or early summer when they become ready, but that of mature plants is at the discretion of the grower. In fact Japanese irises can be planted and transplanted at any time if given proper care, but in the United States this work has usually been done in September. Actually, other conditions being right, the best time to plant is probably soon after the end of bloom. Root growth is active at that time, enabling the plant to become better established before cold weather than it would if planted in September. In Japan it has long been the practice to transplant shortly after bloom has ended; and in the United States as early as 1964 Arthur Hazzard of Michigan recommended that it be done as soon after the bloom period as possible (Hazzard 1964). Nevertheless environmental conditions must be correct. In regions where there are weeks or months of heat and drought after the end of bloom, transplanting must be put off until fall. The fall also is usually more suitable for the commercial grower who must fit that part of the nursery work into the other demands on his time. Transplanting shortly after bloom also presents a problem to the hybridizer who is reluctant to move a plant bearing immature pods. However with care to protect the stalks bearing pods, the plants can be moved without affecting the maturing of the pods. Alternatively, the clump can be divided and the part bearing the pods left in place when the rest is transplanted. Dividing a plant like this *in situ* is easily done. After loosening the soil around the part to be removed, two spading forks are inserted back to back at the center of the clump. One fork holds in place the part to remain and the other separates and lifts out the part to be removed.

Where conditions are correct, the best time for planting Japanese irises is probably shortly after the end of bloom. Otherwise the choice is between spring and fall. Which of these times is better depends largely on climatic conditions. In regions with moderate summers and very cold, early winters, spring is preferable, as planting in the fall does not allow time for sufficient root growth to anchor the plants in their new sites and they are at risk of being lost through heaving during the subsequent freezes and thaws. In the author's garden in

Maine spring has proved to be excellent. In regions with mild winters and hot, dry summers, fall planting is much the better to spare the newly set plants the stresses of summer heat and drought. Indeed, in places where bloom is in the spring or early summer and followed by months of severe heat and drought, and where root growth can be expected to continue well into the winter months, late fall is preferable to September.

Preparing for Dormancy

As fall approaches care must be taken to remove all unwanted seed pods before they can mature and spill seeds. Seeds spilled in that way can give rise to plants which are not what the label claims, resulting in confusion for the grower and, in commercial gardens, the possible sale of incorrectly identified plants. When the leaves have turned brown and are no longer useful to the plant in photosynthesis they should be cut off as close to the ground as feasible and discarded. This avoids the need for cleaning up messy dead leaves in the spring and gets rid of the debris in which pests and agents of disease live over the winter.

Special Methods of Culture

Pot Culture

In Japan, where growing Japanese irises in pots has a very long history, it is practiced far more than in the United States. A major reason for pot culture there has been to make it possible to bring the growing plants indoors to enjoy their beauty and the particular fascination of watching the flowers as they open. Nevertheless Hirao estimated in 1964 that only about 10 percent were grown there in that way.

Hirao has described in detail the technique of pot culture as used in Japan (Hirao 1964) and Craig has detailed his use of it in California (Craig 1967). Soon after bloom has ended the plant is removed from the pot in which it has been growing, the spent leaves are trimmed to about 6 inches, and the plant is divided into single divisions which are individually replanted in pots. Most commonly 4-inch pots are used in Japan but even there 6- to 7-inch pots are preferred for exhibition purposes and this size is usual in the United States. If the plants are to remain in the pots more than one year, 10-inch ones are better. Plastic pots are preferable to clay ones, the pores of which tend to become heavily contaminated with algae. When the water becomes contaminated it should be replaced. Light, acid soil, sphagnum moss, or even boiled sawdust is used as the growing medium in Japan but in the United States a mixture of equal parts of good loam, compost, and dried commercial cow manure (or a smaller amount of well-rotted manure) is preferred. Since the plants will remain in the pots only a year, or at most two, the problem of the new roots coming too close to the surface does not apply, and the crowns need to be no more than ½ inch to 1 inch deep. The pots are placed in water 1 to 2 inches deep and should remain there continuously, since subjecting the plants to alternate water and drought can lead to rot. A plastic wading pool serves well to hold the pots, or pools can be made by constructing wooden trays 3 or 4 inches deep and of any convenient size and lining them with polyethylene sheeting. A hole about 2 inches from the bottom ensures that the water is not too deep. If a pool made of concrete is to be used, the pH of the water must be tested periodically because of the lime in the cement. No fertilizer is used until new growth is 6 inches tall. Craig (1967) advises completely water-soluble fertilizer of acid type and formulas of 10–10–10 or 20–20–20. He adds this directly to the water in the pool starting with a handful and adding more every few days until the leaves are a deep blue-green color. However, all fertilizer is stopped at the first sign of the starting flower buds, as continuing fertilizing at that stage may lead to such softening of the buds that they drop off. Repotting is done right after the end of bloom and no further fertilizer is given until the new growth is 6 inches tall. If growth of algae makes the pools unattractive the water can be changed. In mild climates the plants can remain in the pools all winter, although with reduced water depth. In colder climates water is drained off and the pots heavily mulched to keep the soil somewhat moist and to prevent heaving, or, preferably, the pots can be removed and buried in a prepared bed with a good mulch cover until spring. In the spring after the pots have been returned to the pool, feeding is resumed when the new shoots start and is continued until flower buds first appear. After bloom the clump may be pulled from the pot without disturbing the soil and replanted in a larger one, divided and restarted in pots, or planted in the ground.

In the United States, pot culture is used chiefly for therapeutic purposes to help ailing plants or to make it possible to grow Japanese irises in parts of the country where natural conditions, such as alkaline soil and drought, are unsuitable. A less common purpose is to force or retard bloom.

The temporary use of pot culture is of great value in helping to restore health in Japanese irises which through neglect, drought or other causes are growing poorly in the ground, with dying roots. Indeed, it will result in prompt restoration of healthy growth unless the plant is beyond hope or has a disease or pest problem that requires a more specific treatment. For this type of pot culture the sick plant is lifted, washed, and trimmed of all dead and unhealthy roots and rhizomes. Unhealthy leaves also are removed and the others cut back to about 6 inches, and the remaining divisions are replanted in pots of suitable size and placed in 1 to 2 inches of water (Vogt 1988). A mixture of equal parts of good, and preferably rather heavy garden soil and dry commercial manure serves well as the growing mix. If the mix or water is alkaline it can be adjusted with ferrous sulphate. Do not use additional commercial granular fertilizer in the mix since, combined with the moisture, it can encourage rot. The pots should be placed in a shallow pool, as described above. They are treated at three-week intervals with acid-soluble fertilizer. After a month or so, when the roots have reached the bottom of the pot, the plant can be removed without disturbing the growing medium and planted in the garden. Ouweneel (1972) recommends the addition of a small amount of root hormone (Rootone) to the water when planting Japanese irises with poor roots in soil, and possibly this would be useful in thera-peutic pot culture also.

Pot culture also provides a good means of growing Japanese irises in places where the natural environmental conditions as regards soil pH, summer heat, and drought make regular garden culture difficult. Its usefulness even in desert conditions has been amply proven (Dan-ielson 1984).

Another use for pot culture is in forcing and retarding bloom. Not infrequently it is desirable to have Japanese iris plants bloom earlier than they normally would in order to have them ready for shows timed for flowers that bloom earlier. This can be accomplished if planned well in advance. If potted plants are brought into the greenhouse or indoors under lights at a temperature of 60° F in winter they can be expected to bloom in eighty to ninety days (Ito 1966, Hirao 1984). If lights are used, they should be on sixteen to twenty-four hours daily.

Similarly, bloom can be retarded by keeping plants in a refrigerator at a little above freezing. In experiments by Ito, potted plants thus stored and brought into the garden or, in winter, into a greenhouse bloomed in forty-five to sixty days (Ito 1953). Indeed plants merely stored in the refrigerator without being potted and subsequently planted as desired bloomed similarly but the stalks were shorter and flowers smaller than normal (Ito 1953).

Cold Over-Winter Storage

Plants dug in the fall too late to be planted safely in the ground and perhaps too numerous to be potted conveniently at that time for storing in a protected place can be stored in the refrigerator over the winter. The plants are washed, divided into convenient sizes, and trimmed of spent and damaged roots, and the leaves are cut back to 4 to 6 inches. With a teaspoonful or so of water to provide moisture the entire plant is placed in a tightly closed plastic bag, and stored in the refrigerator at 40° to 46° F. In one such trial in Kentucky all plants removed and planted in either the ground or pots in March to early June lived and grew well, but ones planted later died (Vogt 1988).

The Acid Bed

This term is used to refer to beds made to maintain a soil pH of 5.5 to 6.5 suitable for Japanese irises in regions where the soil and water are naturally in the alkaline range. Broadly speaking, an acid bed might mean anything from one merely treated with acid-producing materials to one painstakingly lined with plastic sheeting to make it a little world of its own quite distinct from its surroundings. The principle is simple. For a large bed remove soil from the selected site, line the excavation thus made with plastic sheeting, and refill the bed with good garden loam of suitable pH. The loam can be enriched with compost and well-rotted manure (about one part to six of loam) and treated with added soil sulfur sufficient to give a pH of 5.5 to 6.0. If the pH is above 7 the sulphur can be applied at the rate of one tablespoon per square yard or one cup per 100 square feet. It takes some three to six months for the sulfur to exert its full effect, so the bed should be prepared well in advance of the time scheduled for planting. In lining the bed a layer of newspapers can be put in first to protect the poly-ethylene sheeting stretched over it. The excavated area should be at least 16 inches deep to ensure that the plastic sheeting will not be torn in subsequent digging. Japanese irises in such a bed should be lifted, divided, and replanted every three years, at which times the bed can be refilled with fresh soil and treated again. Hence, if the total bed is large, it is easier to build it in three separate sections so that one section can be redone each year on a three-year rotation (Delmez 1986).

An additional problem in areas with alkaline soil conditions is that the water supply can be expected to be alkaline also. If only mildly on the alkaline side, treatment of the soil with sulfur will be enough to offset the effect of the water. Under extremely severe conditions with much calcium in the water, the problem has been solved in one garden in the area of Del Mar, California, by the installation of a filtering system in which the water flows between closely spaced plates of copper and magnesium and then through sand (Gunther 1987).

Full-scale acid beds of the sort described above are not common, but similar beds on a small scale are used by many lovers of Japanese irises and other species requiring acid soil and abundant water and are easily made. A 5-foot diameter plastic wading pool will hold a dozen or so plants. Ten or more $\frac{1}{4}$-inch holes are cut around the circumference of the pool about one quarter of the distance from the bottom and the pool is placed in an excavation made for it so that its rim is about 1 inch above ground level. Some charcoal briquets are scattered over the bottom to help keep the water reservoir in the bottom of the pool from souring and the pool is filled to about 2 inches from the top with soil that has previously been treated to suitable acid pH and mixed with compost and cow manure. A mulch fills in the remaining two inches (Wood 1987b).

Still smaller containers can be used, of course, for fewer plants. Indeed, an acid setting in the midst of a bed with soil of alkaline reaction can be improvised for even a single clump by digging a hole some 16 inches deep and of suitable diameter for the plant in question. Well-rotted manure with 4 ounces of soil sulfur is mixed in at the bottom. The hole is then filled with good soil containing another 2 ounces of sulfur. In one trial in a desert location in New Mexico this brought the pH down from the normal 7 to 7.5 of the area to 5.5 to 5 in about six months. Japanese irises planted in this way and receiving abundant water thrived (Danielson 1987).

CHAPTER 6   *Uses*

J APANESE IRISES lend themselves to a wide variety of uses. In the perennial border they go well with other flowers, but they are so spectacular that they put on a very satisfying show by themselves and some growers prefer to combine them with plants that bloom chiefly before or after them. Since they should have acid soil it is well to combine them with other plants that prefer or happily tolerate those conditions. In a mixed border, in which their sword-like leaves contrast well with plants with rounder ones, acid-type fertilizer can be used for the Japanese irises and ordinary fertilizer for plants with less liking for acid conditions. On the other hand if one wishes a border with a single type of foliage, a planting consisting entirely of the very earliest bulbs, crocuses, daffodils, bearded irises, Siberian and Japanese irises and daylilies will give bloom continually from early spring until fall, especially if reblooming daylilies and irises are selected.

Japanese irises make excellent companion plants in a shrub border and are lovely as specimen clumps near a favorite garden bench or beside the mailbox or bird bath. The changing of the water each day and the splashing of water by the birds makes the latter an ideal spot. For landscaping they are unsurpassed as plants along the edges of ponds and streams (plate 28). Planted in pots in shallow pools they are particularly attractive, with their reflections in the water adding to the charming effect. If the garden does not include a natural pond, small pools to hold potted plants can be readily made with a wading pool, large plastic basin, or wooden boxes 3 to 4 inches deep lined with polyethylene sheeting. These can be sunk in the ground with surrounding planting to give a natural effect. An even simpler solution is to dig a depression in the ground of whatever shape one desires and line it with polyethylene, the top edges of which can be buried in the ground. Concrete should be avoided because of its alkaline reaction.

As in planning any perennial bed one must take into account the heights of the various plants, with the taller ones serving as background for those that are shorter. The variations in height of different Japanese iris cultivars makes it possible to select one for any part of the border except the very front—although some promising short miniatures are beginning to appear which may provide plants suitable even for there. Similarly the ultimate size of clumps must be anticipated, but since Japanese irises usually should be lifted, trimmed, and replanted every three or four years, their clump size can be adjusted as part of their general care.

Like most flowers, Japanese irises look better in groups than placed in a row (plate 29). Beds of solid colors can be impressive, as can the infinite variety of mixed color patterns that can be created by including striped, veined and marbled varieties as well as those of solid colors. The judicious use of white Japanese irises is particularly effective. White selfs among the darker ones not only provide accent but tend to blend the planting together as a whole. A few groups of white Japanese irises against a background of shrubs can be the main feature of a shrub border.

The particular companion plants that should be included with Japanese irises must be a matter of personal choice but some may be mentioned as possibilities. For taller background subjects dogwood, flowering cherries and crabs, Japanese maple, fringe tree, silver magnolia and evergreens serve well. In the shrub border azaleas, blueberries, mountain laurel, andromeda and rhododendrons are natural choices, since they too prefer an acid environment, but almost any desired shrub is suitable. Among other perennials, those often used include daylilies, Siberian and other irises, chrysanthemums, asters, *Aconitum napellus* and *fischeri,* astilbes in pink, white, and red, *Doronicum,* columbine, lupins, oriental poppies, coral bells, shasta daisies, sweet william and drummond phlox and, for edging, the low pinks, ajuga, alyssum, and candytuft.

Japanese irises are extremely well suited for landscaping. Gardens created in the Japanese manner (plate 30) have become popular in larger private properties and in botanical gardens and parks. Japanese irises are particularly appropriate in such settings. They also lend themselves magnificently to large landscape projects such as that at the Kyoto Heian Shrine Iris Garden (plate 28). In Japan very large landscape plantings are extremely popular. The huge display at the Tokyo Botanical Garden (plate 31) is an attraction visited by thousands of tourists from other countries as well as countless Japanese. The early gardens, such as the Kotaka-en in Horikiri, the Musashi-en, and many others, were planted in rice-paddylike areas with raised wooden walkways and platforms where the visitors could have tea surrounded by the beauty of the flowers. This practice continues to the present with some of the larger gardens visited by as many as one hundred thousand lovers of Japanese irises yearly. George Reed wrote an excellent account of these gardens as they were in the early decades of the present century (Reed 1931).

The Act

A very special use of Japanese irises in Japan is the ritual of enjoying what is known as the Act. Hirao (1964) has explained that this dates back to the mid-nineteenth century when, in selecting their seedlings, growers became fascinated by the mystery of the movement or act of the flower in opening. On arranging the potted plants indoors to watch the flower open, it was found that they were most beautiful in front of a gold panel.

A well-grown potted Japanese iris suitable for the Act will, when taken into a room at the early stage of bloom, unfold its petals slowly but steadily. During its three-day life the petals enlarge ceaselessly until the afternoon of the third day, with the appearance of the flower changing hour after hour. A true Japanese lover of this ritual will meditate and watch the Act as the beautiful flower slowly opens in front of the golden panel. Hirao remarks that "watching a flower in this way leaves an impression that will last a lifetime" (1964, 36). Sad to say, in recent times interest in this ceremony has decreased, suggesting perhaps a change of taste and tempo of life (Wood 1983).

CHAPTER 7 ※ *Diseases*

MOST GARDENERS are now aware of the hazards as well as the virtues of chemicals used to control diseases and pests—hazards to the environment as well as to themselves—if used carelessly or not as directed by the manufacturer. It is unlawful to use pesticides except on crops and in amounts prescribed by the Environmental Protection Agency. Allowed uses are shown on the label and in the directions that come with the products. Unfortunately, manufacturers have small incentive to apply for registration of their products for use in crops of such small market value as irises. As a result, products that can be extremely valuable to the iris grower and are of only minor toxicity may not be registered for irises. Hence, if the grower has questions about the use of any pesticides mentioned in this book or elsewhere it is recommended that the State or local Department of Agriculture, University Cooperative Extension Service, be consulted as to the advisability of using it.

For only a few of the disease and insect pest problems of Japanese irises is our knowledge very exact. What is said in the following discussions of the various problems has been gathered through personal experience, reading and, especially, through the answers to a detailed questionnaire sent to experienced growers in the United States and other countries.

For convenience the various problems are considered under the headings of diseases in this chapter and of insect and other pests in the next. It must be understood, however, that although a few diseases are of metabolic or other noninfectional causes, most of the ones we recognize in plants are due to what may be thought of as pests of microscopic size: bacteria, fungi, viruses, nematodes, and other tiny organisms.

Diseases Due to Infectious Agents

In the following discussion of diseases a number are mentioned for the sake of completeness which, although serious problems in bearded and some other irises, have not in recent years been known to affect Japanese irises in the United States. Indeed, one of the particularly noteworthy and valuable features of Japanese irises is their freedom from diseases.

Diseases Caused by Bacteria

A number of serious bacterial diseases occur in bearded irises. These include bacterial leaf blight (causative agent *Xanthomonas tardicrescens*) and bacterial soft rot (causative agent *Erwinia carotovora*). According to the listing of plant diseases in the United States published by the United States Department of Agriculture in 1960 these serious diseases affect Japanese irises also, and soft rot is mentioned as occurring in Japan (Hirao 1987, Horinaka 1987, Kamo 1989). Kamo mentions that streptomycin is of some help in combating soft rot, which supports the view that in Japan the disease is of bacterial origin. If this disease occurs in Japanese irises in the United States it must currently be an insignificant problem for neither it nor bacterial leaf blight was recognized as a disease problem by any of the experienced growers in this country whose opinions were solicited.

Diseases Caused by Viruses

A number of iris mosaic viral diseases are known to affect bearded and bulbous irises (Weiler 1978a) but we have been unable to learn of any instance of recognizable viral diseases in Japanese irises.

Diseases Caused by Fungi

Fungi are a major cause in bearded irises of such diseases as crown rot (causative agent *Sclerotium rolfsii*), fungal leaf spot (causative agent *Didymellina macrospora*), rust (causative agent *Puccinia sessilis*), and botrytus rhizome rot (causative agent *Sclerotinia [Botrytis] convoluta*), as well as other less common ones such as blossom blight (causative agent *Sclerotinia [Botrytis] cenerea*) and root rot (causative agents *Rhizoctunia solami* and *Phytophthora*). Of this formidable list none has been identified with certainty in Japanese irises in the United States. Spotty lesions on leaves that may have been rust have been noted

(Ackerman 1989) but a causative agent was not identified. On the basis of current information it seems necessary for the purposes of this book to give further consideration only to botrytis, crown rot and rust.

For many years it was believed that botrytis affected only bearded irises (Jackson 1972, Weiler 1978) but in 1979 it was reported to affect also Siberian irises (Hollingworth 1979) and since that time it has become clear that it can be a serious problem in those irises in the United States, England and the Continent. As yet we know of no occurrences of botrytis in Japanese irises even in large plantings of both Siberian and Japanese irises where it has been a problem of considerable concern among the Siberians (McEwen 1989). Nevertheless, for the present it should be kept in mind as a possibility to be investigated in the case of plants with suggestive symptoms where no other cause is recognized. In Siberian irises the early symptom is the appearance in the spring of greasy brownish patches on the leaves, especially at their bases. The outer leaves of the plant are affected first, and the plant collapses at the base. A gray fungal dusting or feltlike coating may be seen at the base of the collapsed leaves. At an advanced stage shiny black fungal sclerotia several millimeters in diameter may be found on the rhizome and in the surrounding soil. The disease is favored by cool, damp spring weather and is less of a problem under warm, dry conditions as the summer advances. Benomyl (Benlate) 50 W ½ to 1 tablespoonful per gallon of water is effective as a spray and soil drench around the plant. If this is not sufficient the plant can be dug, washed and trimmed of obviously diseased tissues, and then soaked in the solution for a half hour before being replanted in clean soil. Let it be repeated that as yet there has been no report of this disease in a Japanese iris; but the many years that passed before it was recognized in other beardless irises suggests the wisdom of not at once dismissing it as a potential concern to the Japanese iris grower.

Crown rot is another disease that can be extremely serious in bearded irises and is listed by the United States Department of Agriculture (1960) as also affecting some beardless irises including Japanese, but it has not been observed by any of the experienced growers in the United States whose opinions were solicited for this book. It has been mentioned as occurring in southern areas of Japan (Horinaka 1987). What was suspected to be fungal crown rot was seen in a large planting in Maine in the spring of 1983 after a summer and fall of unprecedented drought followed by an extremely cold winter. Many

Japanese irises were dead the following spring and were found to have rotting crowns, rhizomes and roots. However plants still living recovered and it was concluded that the deaths were due not to disease but to the disastrous weather conditions, and that the rot was what would occur in any dead tissue (McEwen 1985).

Iris rust is common in bearded irises. It is not listed in the United States Department of Agriculture Index of Plant Diseases (1960) as occurring in Japanese irises but is suspected from time to time by growers because of the appearance of rusty colored streaks and patches on the leaves; and it is mentioned as occurring in Japan (Horinaka 1987). Such descriptions as we have seen do not, however, fit that of rust due to *Puccinia sessilis* in tall bearded irises with "small, rusty brown lesions over the entire leaf from which erupt spores as fine as dust" (Weiler 1978, 342). Its possible occurrence noted by Ackerman in a Maryland garden has been mentioned above. Hager notes it as a relatively minor and controllable problem in California in bearded irises and some of the non-bearded, especially Louisians, rarely spurias and Siberians, and in the *Californicae* sometimes in coastal areas, but he does not recall it in Japanese irises (Hager 1989). None of the other experienced growers who responded to our questionnaire regarding disease had observed it. Probably most or all examples of what beginning Japanese iris growers suspect to be rust are actually damage due to thrips, which cause rust-colored streaks and patches, however such damage is very different from the small, rounded lesions of rust which smear if touched lightly with a finger. If rust does actually occur it must be rare and not serious. If suspected, proof would require the demonstration of *Puccinia sessilis* in the lesions. Its control in those species in which it has occurred appears to be simple with the newer systemic fungicides such as oxycarboxin, triodimefon or triforine.

Diseases Caused by Nematodes

There are innumerable species of these microscopic worms, many of which are beneficial and others harmful. Of the harmful ones, many live in the soil and may merely cause minor injury as they nibble the roots from the outside. Others live within the roots and it is these that are the most destructive.

The root knot nematode, a *Meloidogyne* species, is the most harmful. It owes its common name to the nodules or "knots" it causes on the roots. The individual nematodes are about $\frac{1}{75}$ inch long and can barely be seen with the unaided eye, but if the knots are cut open, they are readily apparent with a powerful hand lens, as tiny pearllike bodies. When the plant is dug and the roots washed, the swollen knots can easily be seen with the naked eye. The characteristic nodules are not found in roots formed in the late fall, winter, or early spring but appear as the weather becomes warm and therefore can be identified on the roots of plants transplanted in August and September. The infested roots stop growing lengthwise and produce lateral branching of hairlike roots that become so abundant and intertwined that the soil can be cleaned off only by soaking in water and using a strong jet stream. This phase is a very apparent sign of the infestation (Hager 1987). Root knot nematodes are a serious problem in tall bearded and other irises, including Japanese, in California and southern states, but they do not appear to tolerate the cold of northern winters (Weiler 1978, Hager 1972, 1987).

Infestation with the root knot nematode is a serious problem, and very difficult to get rid of. Hager (1987, 1989) has reviewed various measures that have been tried. Use of a nematicide was effective in eliminating from the roots perhaps 80% of the nematodes but the survivors rapidly reproduced and the severity of infestation was very soon as bad as before. Since these nematodes are in the roots only, shaving the roots off right down to the rhizome has been successful with tall bearded irises, which quickly form new roots. Growth of new roots on shaved rhizomes of Japanese irises has been much less certain in Hager's trials and occurred only in some that were shaved soon after the end of bloom when experience has taught that new root growth is very active. Early spring shaving may be suitable also, as root growth is active at that time, but this is still unconfirmed. The shaved rhizomes are planted in pots as described in the section on therapeutic pot culture. Another possible method involves soaking the roots in hot water. Kamo soaks the plant in water at 113° F for thirty minutes, which kills the nematodes but not their eggs, so it must be repeated a month later (Kamo 1989). In Hager's experience this unfortunately has taken a serious toll of killed plants. A fourth method tested by Hager (1987) is based on the principle that nematodes cannot live long in submerged conditions. The plant is grown the year around in clean soil in a container standing in water deep enough to cover the crown two or three inches. This is possible of course only under conditions permitting this type of culture.

In view of the shortcomings of those methods aimed at control of the root knot nematode it is encouraging that successful control appears to be at hand through the use of dimethoate. Hager mentioned preliminary trials of this systemic pesticide in a 1987 article and subsequently has confirmed successful results (Hager 1989). The bare-rooted, washed plant is soaked for one hour in a solution of dimethoate using the manufacturer's directions for the correct proportions for making a solution for a spray or drench. It is then planted in a gallon container filled with soil that has been heat sterilized or fumigated with methyl bromide. The container is then placed in an inch or two of water and grown in that way for a year without allowing the soil to dry out. Hager reports that he has found no evidence of the root knot nodules after the first year, but to be safe he has repeated the procedure a second year before planting in the ground in a bed previously fumigated with methyl bromide. The dimethoate treatment cannot be effectively used merely as a soak for plants in the ground because, obviously, if the plant needs treatment the nematode must be in the soil also, and even if the roots might be temporarily freed of the nematodes they would be promptly infected again.

Further experience is needed to confirm these early trials and to learn more exactly how best to use dimethoate. Hager's results suggest that a single treatment may be sufficient; and it may be that the treated plant can be successfully planted directly into a sterilized bed or will need to be grown in a pot only a month or so as in the method for therapeutic pot culture. It does appear, however, that at last there is a method to control the root knot nematode.

The meadow (or lesion) nematode (*Pratylenchus penetrans*) is another that lives within the roots. It is ubiquitous and has been found in the roots of every iris from all parts of the United States, Europe, and Japan examined in one study (McEwen 1978). It is fortunate, therefore, that it usually does not appear to harm the plant seriously, because it is so widely spread that its control would be extremely difficult. The roots of infested plants show scattered brown and red streaks and look less healthy than those of plants from which these nematodes have been eradicated but in Siberian irises, and presumably also in Japanese irises, plant growth and bloom does not seem to be appreciably impaired (McEwen, 1978). These observations were made in a northern garden; possibly the meadow nematode may be a greater problem in warmer regions (Hager 1987).

It was suspected in 1946 to be the cause of root damage and death in Japanese irises in the New York Botanical Garden (Dodge 1946). In light of what is known about Japanese irises and *P. penetrans* today, however, there is considerable doubt whether the nematodes found were the cause of disease or merely innocent bystanders, since they can be found in the roots of all irises, healthy or sick. The presence of the root knot nematode can be told merely by inspecting the roots but this is not true in the case of the meadow nematode. If root clippings are left in a few drops of water for several hours, the nematodes come out of the roots and can be seen thrashing about in a drop of the water. This however requires the use of a microscope.

Hager (1989) reports that the dimethoate treatment that may work for root knot nematodes appears to be less effective against the meadow nematode. This nematode can be eradicated from a plant by soaking the rhizome and roots in a suitable nematicide such as ethoprop and replanting them in soil fumigated with methyl bromide or other soil fumigant. Soil fumigants, like ethoprop, are all toxic and are restricted for use. A more recently introduced agent for eradication of nematodes in the soil is Cladosan, a chitin product made from shellfish. It does not act on the nematodes directly but by enhancing the effectiveness of protective agents and materials naturally present in the soil. It is a biological product that should be safe to use, but we have as yet no reports regarding its usefulness. Plants freed of the meadow nematode and replanted in fumigated soil will remain free of the nematode for a number of years but eventually the treated beds will be re-invaded from the unfumigated surrounding area. Such a treated, "clean" plant will at once be reinfested if moved to a new location unless the new bed also has been fumigated (McEwen 1978).

Disease Caused by Mycoplasmalike Organisms

Scorch was until very recently considered a disease of unknown cause. A plant disease for which no causative agent has been identified can be diagnosed only on the basis of its symptoms. Lacking the demonstration of a specific causative agent, diagnoses must be based solely on the presence of features which are sufficiently characteristic to make diagnosis reasonably probable. Furthermore, scorch has been defined as it appears in tall bearded irises and it is only an assumption that a disease of beardless irises that has similar features must be the same. The particular features of what is currently diagnosed as scorch are alike in both Japanese and Siberian irises. The affected plant begins to show brown leaf tips and this color gradually involves the entire leaf. A feature that distinguishes scorch from botrytis (in Siberian irises) is that the leaves affected first are those at the center of the plant whereas in botrytis they are the outermost leaves. There is no evidence of fungal dusting of the affected leaves. If the diseased plant is dug the rhizome is found to be firm, but the roots are dead and consist merely of the stringlike central tissue loosely encased in a tube-like sheath, with none of the normally firm root tissue between. There have been a few reports of the recovery of Japanese irises from what has been thought to be scorch, but the disease is almost invariably fatal. It is fortunate therefore that to date the disease has remained one that attacks only an occasional plant. In a large planting of several thousand Japanese and Siberian irises, for example, perhaps only one in four hundred Siberian irises will be affected annually and even fewer Japanese irises (McEwen 1989). Furthermore, plants on each side of a diseased one remain healthy and a new, healthy seedling can be immediately planted in the place where the diseased one was removed, in the same untreated soil, without acquiring the disease. Although this is the usual experience there have been reports of what appeared to be the same disease affecting multiple plants in a bed of Siberian irises although not necessarily the ones next to each other (Hewitt 1987).

In early studies a bacterium, a *Pseudamonas,* was thought by Bald to be the cause of scorch (Bald 1969), but this could not be confirmed by Wadekamper who also was unable to identify a fungus or virus as the cause (Wadekamper 1972). Hence it has been thought of as a disease of unknown cause. However, in 1988 new studies reported that a mycoplasmalike organism had been demonstrated electron-micros-copically in the tissues of tall bearded irises with scorch (Sjolund 1988). These microorganisms, resembling bacteria but lacking cell walls, were seen to be blocking the nutritive conducting cells of the plants, leading to their death from starvation (Sjolund et al. 1989). If this report proves to be correct for Japanese and Siberian irises also—the evidence is fully convincing with regard to tall bearded irises—it will explain the usual lack of spread of the disease and also the occasional reports of spread. Mycoplasmas do not live outside the living tissue cells they infect, hence they would not, like bacteria or fungi, spread directly from plant to plant. They spread only by being carried by insect vectors in whose cells they can live. Hence they would go from one plant to another only if the insect should carry them there. The vector in this case appears to be a leaf hopper (*Cicadellidae*). These sucking insects ingest the mycoplasmas which then live in the cells of the leaf hopper until it deposits them in the cells of the next plant it feeds on. As this book goes to press these studies have not been extended to beardless irises, but one may assume that what has been thought to be scorch in Japanese and Siberian irises will be found to be caused by mycoplasmas also. Studies of possible means of cure are also in progress. Some forms of mycoplasmalike organisms causing disease in humans are susceptible to tetracycline and other antibiotics. Trials of Agristrep, the agricultural form of streptomycin, used to soak the soil around the plant (one treatment weekly for four to five weeks) have been successful in treating bearded irises but have not yet been tried with beardless irises (Sjolund 1989).

Diseases Not Due to Infectious Agents

Nutritional Diseases

Any plants lacking adequate amounts of essential food elements will, of course, grow poorly and if too severely starved will die. Japanese irises need more food than most plants, but this can normally be provided by the appropriate use of fertilizer. There are two particular nutritional deficiencies which result in a similar symptom, namely, an increasing yellowing of the leaves. This can be due either to insufficient nitrogen or to insufficient utilization of iron by the plant (chlorosis), and in both is aggravated by lack of soil acidity. In nitrogen deficiency the entire leaf including the veins is yellow. In chlorosis the veins remain green (except in extremely advanced cases) but between the veins the leaves are yellow. Nitrogen deficiency is readily corrected by use of a high nitrogen fertilizer. An immediate spray with a soluble type fertilizer can be used for its quick effect together with application of a high nitrogen granular fertilizer for its more lasting value.

Chlorosis, a medical term from the Greek meaning green, is used for a form of anemia in which the skin has a greenish tint, but in plants means the nutritional deficiency causing normally green leaves to turn yellow. Korcak lists twelve or more causes of chlorosis but the principal one is iron deficiency (Korcak 1987). Iron is essential in the action of chlorophyll required for photosynthesis by which plants utilize the sun's energy for life and growth. Iron deficiency can result from insufficient amounts of iron in the soil but usually those supplies are adequate and the problem is due to the inability of the plant to utilize iron because of its presence in insoluble form. The soil pH is particularly important. Korcak states that activity of iron decreases a thousandfold for each unit increase in pH so that at pH 7.5 and higher it is completely insoluble in water. Hence the occurrence of chlorosis strongly suggests the need to acidify the soil. A soil test will settle the question.

High amounts of phosphates in the soil such as can occur through the use of large amounts of superphosphate fertilizer (0–46–0) also can cause chlorosis by combining with the iron to form insoluble iron phosphate.

Korcak discusses increased concentrations of calcium carbonate and bicarbonate in the soil as other causes of chlorosis. Calcium is present in the soil as calcium carbonate ($CaCO_3$) derived from limestone and other minerals. Its effect in raising the pH and hence leading to chlorosis in that way is clear. Whether it plays a role in other ways is less certain. Calcium is one of the minor nutritional substances used by plants but too much is harmful. Especially in very moist soil, calcium carbonate combines with carbon dioxide (CO_2) in a chemical reaction releasing calcium and bicarbonate ions (HCO_3) that are harmful to most plants (Marschner 1986).

Chlorosis is easily treated by watering with a solution of iron chelate, purchasable at any garden supply store, according to the maker's directions. Iron in chelated form cures rapidly because it is directly and quickly absorbed into the plant. It does not, however, affect the pH and unless acidifying measures are taken also its effects will not be lasting. Iron (ferrous) sulfate is excellent to use as it adds iron to the soil and is also very effective in increasing its acidity. It is not immediately curative, however, because the iron is not absorbed at once by the plant. If chlorosis has already occurred iron chelate should be used in addition to the ferrous sulfate for its quick effect. If the yellowing of the leaves is due to alkaline soil pH, Rich recommends a drench of tannic acid solution (one part tannic acid to fifty parts water) which she reports will quickly return the leaves to a normal green (Rich 1989).

Some plants are more susceptible to nutritional deficiencies than others, so that only one or two in a bed may at first show the yellowing due to either chlorosis or nitrogen deficiency. This serves as a warning that the whole bed needs appropriate treatment.

Red Roots

Japanese irises contain a red pigment, the exact nature of which is not known, which is responsible for the light red color seen on the cut surface of the rhizome. Normally the roots look white, but at sites of injury the red pigment can ooze out, causing red streaks and spots along the roots. This can happen as the result of a mechanical injury or from damage caused by nematodes, larvae or other organisms. Thus the red spots on the roots do not themselves represent a disease but are an indication of injury.

Accordion Pleating of Leaves

This also is not strictly a disease. Not uncommonly one sees short areas of tight back and forth folding like accordion pleating in a leaf the remainder of which has the normal appearance. This phenomenon occurs in various types of irises, daylilies, and grasses. No tendency has been observed for it to occur in some cultivars more than others and a plant showing it one year is no more likely than any other to do so the next year. It is seen in the central leaves which are the ones growing most rapidly and clearly is due to an abnormality of growth. A plausible explanation relates it to decrease in the lubrication of the leaves. Normally, the more rapidly growing central leaves slide past those enfolding them. With loss of lubrication, cell division, and hence growth, would continue as rapidly as before, but if the new growth could not slip upward it would of necessity fold back and forth until a change in environmental conditions restored lubrication and permitted growth to proceed normally again (Ackerman 1989, Coble 1988). Vogt has observed it in plants growing in the ground but rarely in potted plants in water (Vogt 1987). Certainly it is not a disease and appears not to be genetically controlled. Although somewhat unattractive it is not important except on the show bench.

Summary

In summary, it appears that in the United States Japanese irises are remarkably free of serious diseases with the exception of damage caused by the root knot nematode in parts of the country where it is found. Fortunately, there now appears to be a successful means of control. Scorch is serious for the plants affected but quantitatively it has been a minor problem and current studies offer promise of a cure.

CHAPTER 8   *Insect and Other Pests*

THE COMMENTS regarding legal aspects and toxicity of chemical materials at the start of the preceding chapter on diseases are particularly applicable to the use of the many agents available for control of the pests discussed here. In Table 1 are listed the generic and trade names of the pesticides mentioned in this book and whether they are of systemic or contact type. A generic name is the scientific name for a given material in contrast to the trade names, of which there are often several for the same substance. The generic names are not capitalized but trade names are. In this book the generic names are used and the reader can refer to Table 1 to find the common trade names by which the desired products may be more easily found in the local stores.

Systemic pesticides are absorbed by the plant through the roots and leaves. They do not harm the plant but are poisonous to the pest as it feeds on the plant. They have the important advantage of protecting the plant for the two weeks or more that they remain at adequate levels in the plant tissues. In contrast, pesticides of contact type must touch the pest, and therefore kill only those with which they come in contact at the time of application and for a short period thereafter. Some pesticides such as *Bacillus thuringiensis* products are different from those of true contact type because, although not absorbed through the plant and, hence, not systemic, to be effective they must be ingested by the pest as it eats bits of the leaves coated with the pesticide.

A number of insect and other pests can damage Japanese irises but few are serious and all are controllable. In this chapter the more important and serious ones are discussed first in some detail and the others are then considered briefly.

Serious Pests

Iris Borer

This pest is the larva of the brownish moth *Macronoctua onusta*. It is the principal cause of damage to irises in the eastern and midwestern United States but has been much less a problem in the South and west of the Rocky Mountains, and apparently has not been found in England or on the Continent. A borer mentioned as a pest of Japanese irises in Japan may be different from the one in the United States, since the latter has only one generation a year whereas, in warm places, the Japanese borer may have three (Horinaka 1987; Kamo 1989). The iris borer common in the United States passes through four stages in its life cycle: egg, larva (the borer), pupa, and adult moth. Excellent photographs and descriptions can be found in the chapter by Naegele and Fordham (1978) in *The World of Irises*. In the fall eggs are laid by the moth on stalks and leaves and on debris around the plant. These hatch in the spring and the larvae climb a few inches up the leaves and invade them by chewing small holes. They gradually eat their way down inside the leaf to its base and into the rhizome. In the case of tall bearded irises, the large rhizome may sustain a borer throughout its larval stage but the smaller Japanese iris rhizome is soon hollowed out and the borer moves on to others. The larva is a hairless, light gray or white segmented caterpillar with pinkish tones and a brown head. When it hatches it is only about ⅛ inch long but by August it has grown to 1½ inches long and about ½ inch wide. In the northern states the larva leaves the rhizome in August and becomes a chestnut-brown pupa about ¾ inch long in the soil near the rhizome. This occurs earlier in regions where the growing season starts earlier. After about a month the moth emerges to lay its eggs and the cycle begins again. The moth is a night-flying one and hence not often seen. It is about an inch or more long and dark brown in color with lighter wings.

In the case of the tall bearded irises, the saw-tooth lesions made in the spring on the edges of the leaves can be seen and make possible an early diagnosis, but in Japanese irises these lesions are less apparent,

TABLE I. *Name and Type of Materials for Control of Plant Problems*

Generic Name	Trade Name	Type
Pesticides		
acephate	Orthene	Systemic
Bacillus thuringiensis products	Dipel, Thuricide, Bactospeine	Contact*
carbaryl	Sevin	Contact
diflubenzuron	Dimilin	Contact
dimethoate	Cygon 2E, Rogor	Systemic
disulfoton	Di-syston Dithiosystox	Systemic
fenvalerate or esfenvalerate	Pydrin, Sumicidin, Asana	Contact
flumvalerate	Marvik	Contact
lindane	Lindane	Contact
malathion	Cythion, Malathion	Contact
permethrin	Ambush, Pounce, Talcord	Contact
Fungicides		
benomyl	Benlate	Systemic
metalaxyl	Subdue	Systemic
oxycarboxin	Plantvax	Systemic
thiram	Arasan, Dilsan, Mercuram, Thimesete	Contact
triodimefon	Bayleton	Systemic
triforine	Funginex	Systemic
Nematicides		
ethoprop	Mocap	Contact
fenamiphos	Nemacur	Contact
———	Cladosan**	
———	Vapam	Soil fumigant
methyl bromide	Brom-o-gas	Soil fumigant
Herbicides		
glyphosate	Roundup	Systemic

*Not strictly contact; must be ingested by the insect.
**Acts as a soil conditioner that helps natural protective agents in soil.

and the first recognizable feature may be a yellow leaf at the center of the plant which easily pulls off at the base showing the torn and often blackened end. At that stage a stiff wire thrust down the hole at the base of the destroyed leaf may succeed in killing the borer but if in doubt it is best to dig up the rhizome and examine it carefully, cutting into the damaged place if necessary. If the problem is due to borers this is readily apparent from the hollowed out area in the rhizome and basal leaves. By that time the borer may be quite large and easily found. These borers are cannibalistic so by the time they reach the rhizome usually only one is left. However, there may be one or two more in other rhizomes, so a careful search should be made. By late summer the larvae will have left the rhizomes, leaving only the hollowed-out remains. At that stage the area for a space of about 12 inches around the plant and 12 inches or more deep should be dug up and a thorough search made for the pupae, which are easily identifiable. Destroying the pupae does not, of course, help with the damage already done but is important in reducing the infestation the following year.

Aside from measures mentioned above to kill the borer larvae and pupae mechanically, control is achieved by spraying rather heavily with dimethoate (see table 1) one tablespoon per gallon of water plus a few drops of a commercial spreading agent or detergent when the spring growth is about 4 inches tall. If borer damage the previous year was severe, a second spraying a week or ten days after the first is advisable. Once borers have invaded the garden the spray program should be used for two successive years, but if no evidence of borer damage is found in the second year it can then be stopped if it is being used only against borers. If this is done, a careful watch must be continued and the program resumed promptly if borer damage reappears. If borer damage is not recognized until the borer has reached the rhizome, a heavy application of dimethoate is worthwhile even as late as a week or two after the end of bloom but, of course, is useless after the larvae have left the rhizome to pupate. Two other systemic pesticides that would probably be effective are acephate and disulfoton (see table 1) but we have as yet no experience with them for borers, and disulfoton is more toxic and should be used only with special caution. Currently, dimethoate is the pesticide of choice and we know of no reports of borers becoming resistant to it through repeated yearly use. Some growers prefer, for the first spray, a combination of dimethoate and a contact pesticide such as lindane, permethrin, fenvalerate, or diflubenzuron. The contact pesticides can be used alone, but in that case repeated applications at weekly intervals are required beginning when growth starts in early spring and continuing until the leaves are about 10 inches tall.

In recent years much progress has been made in the use of so-called biologic methods to control pests. Juvenile stage parasitic nematodes (*Neoplectana carpocapsae* and other species) have been recommended for control of borers. These beneficial nematodes parasitize a large variety of larvae and pupae including those of borers while those pests are in the soil, but not after they have started to climb the leaves or have entered them. Hence, their application must be timed either for early spring when the eggs start to hatch or for the later stage of the borer's cycle (about mid-August in the northern regions) when the larvae eat their way out of the hollowed-out rhizome and enter the soil to pupate. Once the population of these nematodes in the soil has been established they should continue to be effective from year to year. In very cold regions, however, they may not survive the winter and a new population may have to be reestablished each spring. As yet this is a new development for control of borers, and also cutworms, on which much more research is needed for a full appraisal of its usefulness.

Other biologic-type products that may be helpful are those derived from *Bacillus thuringiensis*. As has been mentioned, these pesticides must be ingested by the borer, which can happen only during the relatively brief period when the larvae are crawling up the leaves and chewing them preparatory to entering them. Since this product is not systemic it is not absorbed by the leaves but is merely on their surface.

Still another product that may be tried is Diatomacious Earth which, dusted on the leaves in early spring when the larvae are starting to crawl up, can pierce the soft tissues of the pest and cause them to dehydrate.

A useful mechanical device to kill the adult moth stage of the borers is the electronic bug "zapper." The devices should be used only in September and October when the moths are flying. They should be equipped with an electric eye which will turn them off during daylight hours, in order to protect beneficial predators that are attracted to the device in daylight hours to scavenge the carcasses of night-flying insects left on the electrode mesh.

In summary, although it is a pest of potential seriousness that must be carefully watched for, the iris borer is much less a problem in Japanese irises than in other irises. In mixed plantings of tall bearded, Siberian, and Japanese irises, experience to date clearly shows that the borers much prefer the bearded ones, take Siberians as second choice and seldom attack the Japanese if other irises are available.

Thrips

Several types of thrips can affect Japanese irises. The most serious one attacks the leaves, and others of minor concern can spoil the appearance of the blossoms. The iris foliage thrips, *Bregmatothrips iridis,* has a particular predilection for Japanese irises. The eggs, which are laid in the leaves, hatch in early spring. The immature thrips are white and the adults dark brown or black and both stages can be seen together. The adult is about ¹⁄₁₀ inch long and the immature ones somewhat smaller. With the unaided eye they are merely tiny specks that move. With a good hand lens they are seen to be insects with three legs on each side, the posterior two of which curve backward and the front ones forward like arms. The head carries two antennae. Except for their color and size the young and adults look alike.

A few may be seen on the surface of the leaves, but they are mostly in the folds of the leaves at the lower part of the plant where they enfold each other. Hence, they can easily be missed unless the leaves are slightly unfolded. Their presence is made apparent, however, by the rust-colored spots, streaks and patches on the leaves. These tend to be first along the lower edges but if the infestation is not controlled the reddish rusty patches spread and can cover most of the lower half of the leaves, or even higher. The thrips feed by rasping the surface of the inner folds of the leaves. It is probable that the characteristic rusty red color of the areas of injury in Japanese irises is due, at least in part, to the oozing of tissue fluid containing the red pigment characteristic of these plants and which gives the cut surface of a Japanese iris rhizoone its reddish color.

Damage occurs early spring to November. Many generations hatch out in succession, so young and adult forms may be found together throughout the growing season. The eggs remain over the winter in the leaves. Hence an important measure of control is to cut off the leaves close to the ground during fall garden clean-up time, and burn them. Various chemical pesticides are useful. Because the thrips live in the basal folds of the leaves it is essential, especially in the case of contact sprays, to direct the spray downward at the base of the plant to help the liquid work its way down between the tightly folded leaves. Because of the uncertainty of reaching the insects with a contact type of spray, the systemic pesticide dimethoate is especially recommended. A spray of one tablespoonful per gallon of water plus wetting agent when the leaves are about 3 to 6 inches tall will serve two purposes, controlling iris borers as well as thrips. A single spraying of dimethoate usually is insufficient and thrips damage is seen again later in the season. This may be due to a failure of the pesticide to kill all the young and adult thrips or, usually, to the hatching of another generation. A second spray can be given two weeks after the first and certainly should be at the first reappearance of thrips. They should be looked for periodically in the basal leaf folds. Dimethoate is the systemic pesticide most commonly used but the other two listed in table 1, disulfoton 15% in granular form and acephate, can be used with success also (Miller 1988, Coble 1987b). If disulfoton is selected particular care must be taken as it is potentially more toxic to the user than are the others, although care in following the directions of the manufacturer is essential for all. Instead of a systemic pesticide, or in addition to it, carbaryl or any of the other contact pesticides listed in table 1 can be used. The combination of a systemic insecticide plus several weekly applications of a contact pesticide with a wetting agent is recommended if either alone is unsuccessful. A dusting of Diatomacious Earth in the folds of the leaves may also be tried.

The thrips that damage the blossoms are a different species (probably *Frankliniella tritici*) related to gladiolus and rose thrips. They cause injury by rasping the petals, leaving the same characteristic flecking seen in damage due to thrips in other flowers. Damage to blossoms varies greatly from place to place and year to year. In one year the infestation in one Michigan garden was so severe that blooms could not be photographed because of hundreds of thrips covering the petals (Coble 1988). Usually, however, damage to flowers is minor and in many gardens it has never been observed.

Pests of Special Concern to Hybridizers

There are several insects which do not threaten the life of Japanese or other irises but spoil the blooms and can be a threat to the hybridizer. These include several which eat the developing seeds, and others which destroy the anthers and stigmas so the flower cannot be used for crossing.

Seed Eaters

The verbena bud moth, *Endothenia hebesana,* is a small brownish-gray moth about ¾ inch long. It lays its eggs on the surface of young seed pods and the hatched larvae bore through the wall of the pod and eat the developing seeds. The holes are very small and become obscured as the pod grows, and hence are rarely recognized. The insect pupates inside the pod and just before becoming a moth, the pupa makes a larger hole and forces itself partway out. The moth emerges leaving the pupal casing still protruding from the pod. There are several broods each year. It is distributed throughout the United States.

The iris weevil or snout beetle, *Mononychus vulpeculus,* is another pest of minor concern except to the hybridizer. It is a brownish-gray beetle about ⅕ inch long with a distinctive snout or beak. The eggs are laid inside the ovary of the plant through puncture holes made in the walls by the snout of an adult, which also feeds on reproductive parts of the blossom, causing disfigurement. Both larvae and pupae develop in the seed capsule which the adult leaves when it opens naturally. The adult has wings and flies if disturbed.

In mixed plantings of Japanese irises involving *I. siberica, I. virginica* and *I. versicolor* its chief damage is to these three (Coble 1988) but it can be a problem in Japanese irises also (Westmeyer 1987). That it is a lesser problem in the Japanese irises may be because of timing as there is only one generation a year and its period of damage may be largely over by the time the Japanese iris seed pods are forming.

Vogt reports that the spathes appear to be essential to enable these insects to enter the seed pods. He removes the spathes as soon as it is clear that the cross has been successful and has observed no damage to the developing seed pod if this is done (Vogt 1988).

Grasshoppers, usually a friendly resident of gardens, can in some situations be a major cause of damage not only to foliage but to seed pods of Japanese and Siberian and other irises (Coble 1988).

Anther and Stigma Eaters

A fly, *Orthochaeta dissimilis,* has been a problem in Siberian irises in Massachusetts (Tiffney 1978). It has been observed also in Maine in Siberian irises but not in Japanese irises (McEwen 1989) and it is as yet not known how widely it is distributed nor what threat it may be to Japanese irises. The larva is an elongated, cone-shaped, smooth white creature about ⅛ inch long with a small black dot at the pointed end and the larger end rather flat. The larva of the fly is found inside the unopened bud where it eats petals and reproductive parts of the flower which, on opening, is spoiled both in appearance and for hybridizing. The small white maggots later crawl out of the blossoms into the spathes where they continue eating pedicel tissue and pupate within the spathes. The adult fly emerges the next spring.

The iris borer, already discussed, can cause damage not only by its more familiar way of destroying rhizomes but also by chewing and weakening stalks so that flowers and pods may be lost, and they occasionally invade blooms where they can ruin the flower for crossing.

Earwigs (Forficula auricularis), a common garden pest, are a very real problem in some gardens with one or two found deep in the throat of perhaps a third or more of the Japanese iris flowers. In many such blossoms the anthers and styles are cut and useless (McEwen 1989). The earwigs can be caught using a pair of long, slender tweezers but they can move with surprising speed and one must be deft and quick. A dusting of carbaryl on the ground and base of the plant helps provide protection. Boards placed on the ground attract earwigs, which collect under them at night and may be sprayed with carbaryl or diazonon (0.5%) in the morning.

Corn ear worms are also an occasional problem in some gardens where they enter flower buds before they open. This active phase of their cycle is apt to be over by the time the Japanese irises are in bloom and they therefore are probably less likely to cause damage in Japanese irises than in ones that bloom earlier (Coble 1988).

Control of the seed eaters and damagers of anthers and styles is difficult. A spray of dimethoate may poison these pests, but since the plant tissue must be eaten before the pest is affected much of the damage will already have occurred. Nevertheless, killing the insects does some immediate good and helps lessen the problem the next year. Because invasion by the pest is often difficult to observe until it has caused damage, a contact spray is probably useful only as a preventive measure with applications at weekly intervals starting as the flower bud begins to form. An important measure, especially in the case of the fly, borers, and earwigs, is daily inspection of the opening flower and hand picking any of the culprits found. Important also for future seasons as well as the current one is cutting and burning (not putting on the compost pile!) all unwanted seed pods, making sure to cut the stalk below the spathe.

Miscellaneous Pests

Cut Worms are a threat to newly planted small seedlings, which they may cut off close to the ground. Usually the seedling will start growth again but is, of course, severely set back. Often the cut worms can be found near a damaged seedling by digging a few inches deep. If one has only a few such seedlings they can be protected with rings of cardboard. The central cardboard spool of a toilet-tissue or paper-towel roll cut into sections serves conveniently for this protection. Carbaryl powder or granules scattered around the seedlings is helpful. Parasitic nematodes (see the discussion of borers) used in the spring before the seedlings are lined out and Diatomacious Earth scattered on the ground around the plants may be useful. Cut worms cause no significant damage to mature plants.

Spider Mites (*Tetranysus telarivs*) are a rare problem but if numerous can cause havoc to newly sprouted seedlings (Coble 1987b). They were readily controlled with Kelthane but that pesticide is no longer available and, as yet, we lack experience with other miticides.

Aphids may be present occasionally on Japanese irises but have not been recorded as a problem by any of the growers whose experience forms the main information in this chapter.

Leaf Hoppers have become a concern as possible threats only since they have been assumed to be the insect vectors involved in the disease scorch discussed in the preceding chapter. They do not cause significant harm to irises directly but only as the vehicle that carries to the plant the mycoplasma-like organisms that cause the disease.

Ants are common in many gardens and are not harmful unless they build a large nest under the crown of a clump.

Other pests of usually minor importance include June beetles, rose chafers, and Japanese and false Japanese beetles which can spoil the beauty of blossoms and are a threat also to roots and rhizomes through their larval grubs in the soil.

Larger Pests

Damage caused by slugs and snails varies greatly in some years and places and can be a major problem, merely an annoyance, or no concern at all. Slugs can climb up stalks on wet nights and chew holes in blossoms but their chief damage is to the leaves. They are especially dangerous to young seedlings which they can eat to the ground; in larger plants they can cause harm but are not lethal. One disadvantage of a mulch is that it provides an ideal habitat for them. A first-line control measure is hand picking (using rubber gloves unless one does not mind disgustingly slimy hands), dropping them in any killing liquid such as strong salt solution. In mulched beds the mulch can be lifted to reveal slugs underneath. In unmulched areas boards placed on the ground will attract the slugs, which can be found under them and sprinkled with salt. A number of slug baits are on the market but care should be taken that pets cannot eat them. A measure found to be highly effective at the Department of Agriculture Research Center at Beltsville, Maryland, is to sink shallow pans in the ground so that edges are at close to ground level and fill them with stale beer. The slugs are attracted to the beer, fall in and drown.

The damage caused by mice, moles, voles, shrews and gophers also varies greatly in different places and can sometimes be serious (Ackerman 1988). Moles cause no direct harm but they are insectivors and their tunneling in search of grubs can cause injury; and mice using the tunnels can directly attack roots and rhizomes. Traps and baits are useful but probably most effective of all is a garden cat.

Rabbits are said to harm the tender leaves of small seedlings but do not seem to care for larger plants, and inquiries have elicited no reports of serious damage.

Continuing up the scale of size, deer are a problem only to a few growers, but they do sometimes eat the tops of mature Japanese and other iris plants and, if the seedling bed is in their path, some seedlings can end up planted very deep indeed. (The same complaints can be lodged against the neighbors' loose cow.) Deer can be deterred by hanging up bars of strong soap and old nylon stockings stuffed with clippings of human hair.

Finally we come to the problem of the garden visitor who does not know the rules of good garden manners. One should not hesitate to ask that handbags, camera bags and the like not be carried into the rows. Fortunately most garden visitors today are sufficiently experienced and thoughtful to make some of the horrors of the past rare, but one still must watch for the ignorant shutterbug who will take off a spent blossom, ignoring its tag marking a cross, in order to have a neat picture of the pretty flower behind it. Fortunately today's fashion style does not encourage the garden visitor to wear the wide loose skirts common some years ago. One can still remember with dismay the havoc caused when a visitor in one of those "ballerina skirts" turned quickly. The billowing, twirling skirt could take off a dozen blossoms. With fashion's trend to narrower skirts and, especially, slacks the problem of inappropriate dress has rarely been a danger in recent years and the main hazard continues to be the dangling bag with, as runners up, unsupervised small children and unleashed dogs.

CHAPTER 9   *Hybridizing*

T HE FELLOWSHIP of gardeners—as distinct from botanists and other scientists concerned with plants—tends to include three large groups: those who love to look at and grow beautiful and useful plants, those who specialize in and collect particular types of plants, and those whose chief interest is helping to create new examples of their favorite plants. This chapter is addressed to the last, the hybridizers of Japanese irises. The hybridizer may be defined as one who purposefully crosses one plant with another to produce hybrids. Theoretically this should exclude those who merely collect and plant seeds resulting from natural crosses in which they played no part. In practice, however, the term is used broadly to include them also. Similarly the definition of a hybrid has undergone modification over the years. A century ago a hybrid was defined strictly as a plant or animal coming from a cross of two different species. Today the definition has been broadened in horticultural usage to include any plant resulting from crossing parents having different genes. This covers any crosses of different plants, even sister seedlings. Theoretically, it should exclude seedlings resulting from selfing a flower with its own pollen but in practice even those are today generally thought of as hybrids.

Planned versus Natural Crosses and Goal Selection

There are two approaches in developing new plant and flower types among Japanese irises: natural crosses in which seeds from open-pollinated flowers (fertilized by insects) are gathered from plants showing desirable characteristics, and controlled crosses in which flowers of a desired plant are purposefully crossed with pollen of

another desirable plant. The harvesting and planting of open pollinated seeds has been done by man since long before the time of
recorded history. Purposeful cross pollination has also been practiced
since ancient times. In Assyria, for example, although there was no
understanding of the sexual and genetic nature of plants, it was known
that the date tree, for example, had to be cross pollinated to bear fruit.
This is illustrated in figure 12.

Certainly, there is nothing wrong with planting open pollinated
seeds, and by continual selection of plants showing desirable traits
through many generations specific goals can be reached. However,
with highly variable species, such as the Japanese iris, it severely limits
the amount of control a person has in obtaining specific objectives.
Naturally, when the plant breeder carefully selects both seed and pollen parents with the specific goal of combining desirable characteristics
from each in individuals among the resulting seedling population,
there is far less chance of having undesirable traits appear from some
unknown pollen source. The challenge here is to determine what desired characteristics might be combined in a complimentary way into
individual seedlings. Far more can be accomplished in a shorter period
of time if specific goals (such as blue flowers uncontaminated with
violet or purple, or excellent branching or repeat bloom) are set ahead
of time and a careful evaluation is made of available parents that may
provide the means for accomplishing that objective. All plant breeders
depend on a certain amount of luck to succeed, but in all probability
more will be accomplished from careful planning than from mere
random crosses among "nice-looking" flowers. The real art in plant
breeding is to set realistic goals and have the insight to determine
which parents make the best combinations to achieve those goals.

Goal selection is largely dependent upon personal concepts of what
constitutes better Japanese irises. Thus, any list of suggested goals is
a subjective one. However, there are certain deficiencies among existing Japanese iris cultivars that are widely recognized. With this in
mind, a person starting to hybridize Japanese iris might consider the
following:

1. "New" colors such as uncontaminated blues, pinks, and reds.
Also, the introduction of yellow into standards and falls (presently,
yellow is confined to the signals except in wide-cross hybrids with *I.
pseudacorus*).

FIGURE 12. Assyrian relief from the palace of Ashurnazïrpal about 880 B.C. at what is now Nimrud showing a winged genie fertilizing a date tree. Presumably, the pail in the left hand holds the pollen. The cone-shaped object in the right hand probably has symbolic meaning as well as serving to dust on the pollen. The Nelson-Atkins Museum of Art, Kansas City, Missouri (Nelson Fund).

2. Cultivars with better, wide-angle branching habits, and with more flowers per stalk.

3. Flowers with greater flower petal substance (possible through tetraploid lines).

4. Longer-lasting flowers.

5. Flowers with multiple parts.

6. Plants with a longer blooming season.

7. Short (miniature or dwarf) forms with flowers of good quality and size appropriate to the height.

8. Plants with unique leaf characteristics, such as intense dark green pigmentation, narrow leaf forms, or variegated leaves.

9. Fragrance.

10. Tolerance to alkaline conditions.

Basic Principles

The iris flower is bisexual: that is, it has both male and female reproductive organs. The major parts of the basic flower (the single flower) come in sets of threes: three falls, three standards, three style arms, three stamens, and so on. Figures 13 and 14 show these parts. The female reproductive organ consists of the ovary, which is divided into three compartments (locules), each of which is extended upward into a separate style ending near its top in a special organ, the stigma, the function of which is to receive the pollen. The male reproductive organ consists of the anther, which bears the pollen, borne on a stalk or filament. The other flower parts, the falls and standards, function as the plant's way of attracting insects to initiate pollination. The signals, located at the base of the falls and just below the curved, anther-bearing filaments and style arms, are exactly what the name implies. They serve as the flower's signal to pollinating insects of exactly where to land and enter the flower for nectar—and although the insect, presumably, doesn't care about hybridizing—for the most effective route to pollinating the flower.

A flower of single type has been used in figures 13 and 14 but the reproductive structures are basically the same in the other types. In the multipetaled flowers, however, in which the extra petals come from conversion of stamens and/or style arms, the stigmas may be absent or vestigial and the anthers attached to the petals without any filament. The hybridizer often has to take particular pains in attempting to cross

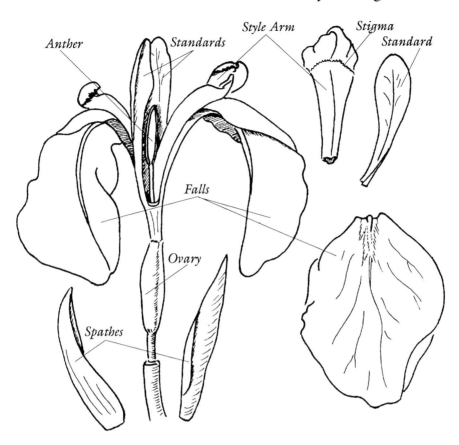

FIGURE 13. The anatomical parts of a Japanese iris flower with one standard, style, and fall removed to show the stamen and anther which lie between the style and fall. The removed style is drawn vertically to show its under (outer) side, with the style crest at the top and just below it the stigma. The two spathes have been removed to reveal the ovary.

the multipetaled flowers and, although rarely, it is sometimes impossible.

The main need in making controlled crosses is to get to the flower and fertilize it with the desired pollen before insects can fertilize it. To obtain the nectar it needs for food, the bee forces its way down to the base of the flower between the fall and the anther and style arm. Its furry back will self the flower with its own pollen if the anther has dehisced (opened to release the pollen) or cross it with pollen it carries from other flowers visited previously. All that is needed to make a controlled pollination is to obtain mature pollen from the desired male parent and place it on the stigma of the desired female parent, using techniques that prevent intrusion by the insects. In this way one knows both parents rather than just the female, or pod parent. Fertilization takes place when the pollen forms a long, microscopically narrow tube which grows down inside the style arm, the nucleus of which then unites with an egg cell in the ovary. Evidence of successful fertilization can usually be detected within a week by the swelling and growth of the ovary after the flower withers. As the season progresses, the ovary develops into a mature seed capsule or pod. Iris seed capsules contain many seeds—each the result of an individual pollen grain fertilizing an individual egg cell.

Basic Procedures

The first criterion is to use only flowers that have not already been visited and fertilized by insects. Unopened flowers at what is termed the balloon stage (the bud expanded into a balloon shape shortly before opening) are the best candidates for making crosses. The stigmas do not become receptive until the flower is ready to open or shortly thereafter. Thus, pollinating very immature buds just showing color and not ready to open for a day or two, will result in very low percentages of fertilized flowers.

The second step in the process of hand pollination is flower emasculation by removing the anthers. Most Japanese iris flowers are self-compatible, that is, they are capable of being fertilized by their own pollen. Hence, one must eliminate this possibility. To do this, gently pull the falls back one by one from the balloon-stage bud, reach in under each style arm with forceps and grasp each stamen and remove it. Some hybridizers leave the falls and standards intact, while others simply snap them off near their bases (leaving the spathe valves intact for support of the ovary) to make access to the stamens easier. Removal of the falls and the standards although seemingly quite brutal, does not appear to reduce the percentage of successful crosses. It also has the added advantage of making the flowers unattractive to pollinating insects so that it is not considered necessary to cover them following hand pollination.

Flower pollination involves placing the desired pollen on the stigma. In the Japanese iris flower the stigma is located in a fold at the end of the style arm on its outer side as shown in figures 13 and 14. The immature, unreceptive stigma is tightly closed against the style arm but when receptive for crossing it can be seen to have opened (figure 14, C, C1, D, and D1).

Either fresh or stored pollen may be used. For fresh pollen the anthers need to be at the dehiscent stage with their pollen seen dotting its surface as shown in Figure 14 at B. Stamens with dehiscent pollen may be gathered the day they are to be used, provided they have been protected against contamination by foraging insects. The anther, grasped near its base, may be used much like a small brush over the receptive stigma.

The method used for storing pollen depends on how long it is to be kept. If for only a day or two, the anthers need merely be placed in small gelatine capsules or envelopes, or even in a small dish in a dry place. If, however, it is to be kept for some time, more elaborate measures are required. Since moisture is harmful to stored pollen, drying is important. This can be easily done by placing the anthers in a small dish in a dry place for several hours until dry and then transferring them and any pollen that has fallen off to small gelatine capsules in which a few small pin holes have been made, or to envelopes, and placing these in screw-top jars containing an inch or so of anhydrous calcium chloride or other drying agent. Anhydrous calcium chloride can be obtained at the local drugstore, or the pharmacist may give without charge a collection of the packets containing silica jell or other drying agents which come from the wholesale supplier with many medicines and are usually discarded. With the lid screwed tight, the jar can then be stored in the refrigerator for several weeks, or in the freezer where the pollen will remain useful for months. The temperature at which the dried pollen is stored makes a profound difference. In one study in which pollen was stored over calcium chloride as dehydrating agent, that stored at 77° F remained useful with about 80% viability for one month, that stored at 32° F for four months, and that stored at −4° F for twelve months. Indeed, after that length of time viability was essentially the same as fresh pollen (Yabuya 1983).

A soft, fine brush may be used to transfer dry stored pollen from the vial to the stigma of the desired pod parent but this is wasteful of pollen unless many flowers are to be crossed with the same pollen, because the brush must be cleaned with a 70% alcohol solution and allowed to dry completely between any changes in pollen parent. A

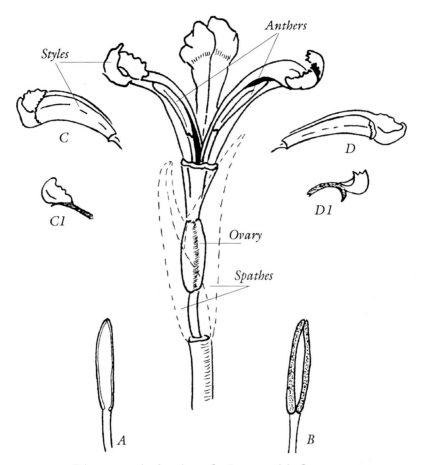

FIGURE 14. Diagrammatic drawing of a Japanese iris flower, dismembered to show the reproductive organs. Below on the left, at A, is an immature, undehisced anther and on the right, at B, one that has dehisced, showing the pollen dotting its surface. Above on the left, at C, is a style with the immature stigma still held against the style, and on the right, at D, the style with stigma open and receptive. C1 and D1 show smaller drawings of the styles viewed from the side to show more clearly the unopened stigma at C1 and the receptive, open one at D1. The position of the removed spathes is shown in dotted lines to illustrate the manner in which they surround and support the ovary and, subsequently, the developing seed pod.

less wasteful technique is merely to cover the mouth of the vial with the index finger and shake until some pollen adheres to the fingertip. The finger is then used as though it were a brush but it too must be cleaned with alcohol between crosses. Another simple method which is most economical in the amount of pollen wasted is to use a wooden toothpick which can be discarded after the cross has been made. A few toothpicks can be prepared in advance by breaking off the tip, leaving a frayed end. Still another simple method if the dried anther remains with the collected pollen is to use it with the pollen clinging to it. It can be replaced with the pollen to be used again.

If the falls and standards are not removed at the time of pollination, the flowers should be covered immediately to prevent subsequent insect pollination. Some hybridizers use inverted paper bags. Others use old nylon stocks cut off to size, or fine nylon netting. Plastic bags should not be used, since they accumulate heat in the sun, collect moisture, and encourage mold growth. The bags may be removed after the flower has withered, and used over again.

In addition to the methods cited, many other techniques are used by individual hybridizers. Two of these are described here. In the author's preferred method the flowers, opened by hand at the balloon stage, have merely the standards and anther-bearing stamens removed and the falls can then be lifted up over the style arms at their tips and tied at the top with a strip of the plant's own leaf. Prior to tying up the falls, the removed stamens can be placed, anther end down, in the central cup formed by the three style arms. Since the stigmas are at the tips of the styles on their outer sides the anthers are safe there until they are ready to be used on some other selected flower. Tying the falls up in this way has the added advantage in hot weather of keeping the pollen more effective for crossing. Later that day or next day when stigmas and pollen are mature the falls are untied, the cross made with pollen from the other parent, the stored anthers used to cross some other prepared flower, and the falls then tied up again.

Another method has the advantage of avoiding the need to prepare the flower and store anthers for use later that day or the next. In this method the buds at balloon stage of the two flowers selected for the cross are opened by hand and the anther-bearing stamens carefully removed. At this stage the anthers probably have not dehisced fully and the stigmas may still be tight against the style arms. With a sharp toothpick used along the line of the anther where it opens, pollen can be picked up. The unopened stigma of the flower selected to be the pod parent can also be gently lifted with the toothpick and the pollen deposited on it. The falls can then be brought up and tied. This method depends on the ability of the pollen and the stigma to mature after the cross has been made. The percent of successful crosses with this method appears to be satisfactory, and its advantage is that the whole procedure of the cross can be completed quickly at one time (Schafer 1989). This method can be used with buds that have not reached the balloon stage if time is pressing but the less mature the stigmas and anthers are the less likely one is to have a successful cross.

Each hand-pollinated cross must be labeled, writing on the label whatever minimal data the particular hybridizer chooses. Usually this includes the date, the serial number of the cross, and the parents, entering the pod parent first. This information is recorded also in the record book together with any other data desired. Many more crosses are made than result in pods but, nevertheless, the information is useful for one's record keeping. The label must be placed below the ovary where it will not restrict the developing seed capsule. Especially in places with heavy rains and high winds small plastic tags are much better than cardboard ones which, softened by rain, can tear off. Short, flexible wires are more convenient than string for fastening the tag.

Fertilization occurs when the microscopic pollen tubules grow down inside the style arms from the stigmas to the ovules in the ovary, a distance of several centimeters. Amazingly, this distance is traversed in only a few hours, and therefore rain occurring after some hours is no cause for concern. A heavy rain shortly after pollination, however, can literally wash out the cross. A rain storm can also render useless a bud that has been opened by hand and prepared for crossing the next day. A useful means of preventing rain damage is to cover the flower with a plastic sandwich bag fastened around the stalk with a tie or a strip of leaf. (A word of caution: If the sandwich bag is of the common fold-lock type, it is essential to cut or tear off the fold, otherwise it fills with water and becomes so heavy that it can break the flower off.) As soon as danger of rain is past the bag is removed before accumulated heat and condensation moisture can harm the flower.

Mature seed capsules split open, exposing the seed for dispersal. Harvesting should take place before this happens. A good rule of thumb is to harvest when the stalk directly below the capsule has changed color from green to light tan. If it is impractical to check the plants during this time on a regular basis, an alternative is to bag the capsules with some material like nylon netting to catch the seeds before they are lost.

Data recorded each season can be valuable for reference purposes. Some parents with handsome flowers consistently produce seedling populations of poor quality. These you will want to avoid in future crosses. Other cultivars are successful as pod parents but not as pollen parents or vice versa. A simple coding system can provide information regarding the pedigree of any seedling and provide a means for judging the value of past crosses. For the serious hybridizer making many crosses each year, a computer can be of aid.

Wide Crosses

The beginning hybridizer should confine himself to intraspecific crosses (crosses within a single species). In the case of Japanese irises this would, of course, be within *Iris ensata*. It must be emphasized, however, that tetraploids can be expected to cross successfully only with other tetraploids. Theoretically, crossing tetraploids and diploids can produce sterile triploids but as yet none are known to have occurred in Japanese irises. Wide or interspecific crosses (that is, between two species) require a great deal of patience and fortitude. Making even a very large number of crosses between two different species gives no assurance that any useful seeds will be formed. Yet, it is among interspecific crosses that the greatest possibilities exist for exotic genetic variations, new flower colors, and other features.

Although there are few general rules of advice for the would-be interspecific hybridizer, there are certain pitfalls to be avoided. First, the genus *Iris* is a very large one, encompassing several hundred species distributed among four large subgeneric groups, each, in turn, divided into sections, subsections and series. The Japanese irises lie within section *Spathula*, subsection *Apogon*, series *Laevigatae*. The closer the genetic relationship between two species, the greater the possibilities are of obtaining valid interspecific crosses. Thus, theoretically, species within series *Laevigatae* are much more likely to hybridize with each other than, for example, a species from *Laevigatae* with a species from series *Spuriae*. The possibility would be even much more remote with a species from a different subsection.

A second consideration is the chromosome make-up of the two species involved. *Iris ensata* is a diploid species with two sets of twelve chromosomes (the basic number is $N = 12$) making a full complement of twenty-four chromosomes. *Iris pseudacorus,* another within the series *Laevigatae,* also has twenty-four chromosomes and it therefore is a logical one to try with *I. ensata.* In fact a number of successful crosses have been achieved between *I. pseudacorus* and *I. ensata* (Tomino and Sakurai 1972; Yabuya 1984, 1985a) but chiefly by using the former as the pod parent. Tomino (1963) reported 40% successful crosses using *I. pseudacorus* as the pod parent but only 14% by the reverse cross, and Kamo reports success only with *I. pseudacorus* as the pod parent. The resulting flowers have been chiefly yellow, with form similar to Japanese irises and markings resembling those of *I. pseudacorus,* but some from crosses made by Ichie and Kamo have included a near-white with blue halos (plate 26), yellow with dark veins, a bicolor of yellow and brown, cream with lavender veins, yellow with crimson sanding, and a lavender-pink self (Kamo 1989). Unfortunately, thus far all these hybrids tend to have yellowish-green leaves and are not vigorous growers. Yabuya's chromatographic analyses of the parent species and the resulting seedlings indicate that the yellow carotenoid pigments of *I. pseudacorus* are dominantly expressed over the reddish anthocyanin pigments of *I. ensata* (Yabuya 1984). Several yellow cultivars from these crosses, such as "Aichi-no-kagayaki" and "Kimboshi" are now quite widely distributed. Unfortunately, as in the case of most wide-cross hybrids from diploid parents, all are sterile.

Still less likely to be compatible are species within the same series but with different chromosome numbers. Most efforts to cross Japanese irises with *I. laevigata,* which has thirty-two chromosomes (two sets of sixteen), have been failures but some successes have been reported. Tomino had one successful cross in three trials using *I. laevigata* as the pod parent but none in ten trials by the reverse cross (Tomino 1963). More recently Yabuya and Yamagata (1980) and Kamo (1989) have obtained seedlings from crosses of *I. laevigata* by *I. ensata.* These hybrids are sterile. That of Kamo has leaves like *I. laevigata* and double, purple, rather large flowers resembling those of Japanese irises. The failure to produce viable seeds appears to be due to degeneration of endosperm in the developing embryos following fertilization (Yabuya and Yamagata 1980; Yabuya 1984). This also appears to be the cause of sterility in the previously mentioned hybrids from diploid crosses of *I. pseudacorus* by *I. ensata* (Yabuya 1985a).

The sterility of hybrids resulting from interspecific crosses of diploid parents is well known in other irises also, for example, the so-called Cal-Sibes from crosses of Pacific Coast species and species of the forty-chromosome group of Siberian irises (subseries *Chrysographes*). Tamberg, however, has obtained fertile seedlings using tetraploid parents (Tamberg 1985). Similarly, Yabuya has obtained fertile hybrids from crosses of tetraploids (amphidiploids) of *I. laevigata* by *I. ensata* (Yabuya 1985b). He also has obtained tetraploid (amphidiploid) hybrids from crosses of *I. pseudacorus* by *I. ensata* which presumably will prove to be fertile also (Yabuya 1989).

Yabuya's chromatographic analyses of the fertile hybrids from *I. laevigata* by *I. ensata* have revealed only the same anthocyanin pigments that are in the parents, and those of both parents also are the same (Yabuya 1987). Hence, these new fertile plants do not show promise of introducing new colors in Japanese irises. It is to be hoped, however, that they can contribute genes for other important features such as early and long-continuing bloom, both of which are characteristics of *I. laevigata*. Clearly, also, if the tetraploid hybrids from *I. pseudacorus* by *I. ensata* prove, as expected, to be fertile, the way will be opened to breeding for yellow and perhaps other new colors.

Continuing with the problem of differences in chromosome numbers in selecting parents for interspecific crossing, such polyploid species as *I. virginica* with 54, 56, and 70 chromosomes, and *I. versicolor* with 72, 84, and 105 chromosomes would seem to be even less likely partners to cross with *I. ensata*. Nevertheless, success has been reported with *I. virginica* as pod parent using embryo culture (Yabuya 1985a).

A third consideration for compatibility in interspecific crosses is the length of the style. Pollen from a species with short style arms is less likely to fertilize flowers of a species with long style arms since the microscopic pollen tubules may not be long enough to reach the ovules.

Inheritance Patterns

The genetic makeup of Japanese irises is complex and the species is highly heterozygous. This is both an advantage and disadvantage to the hybridizer. The advantage is that there is a great deal of variability among seedling populations of almost any cross the hybridizer may make. This opens up a wide spectrum of colors, forms, and other features, from which to make choices. The disadvantage is that the patterns of inheritance of various characteristics, for example flower color, are very difficult to predict.

There are a few inheritance patterns about which we are reasonably certain, which can provide valuable tools for the hybridizer. For example, the single Japanese iris flower is genetically dominant over double-flowered forms. This is not surprising, because it is the form of the wild species. Plants with single flowers may be homozygous, with both genes acting toward development of single flowers, or heterozygous, with genes for both singleness and doubleness present. Therefore, when one crosses two plants with single flowers, one may obtain all singles, if either plant is homozygous, or a three-to-one ratio of singles to doubles if both parents are heterozygous. Double flower forms are recessive. When one crosses two double-flowered plants, all the progeny should also be double flowered. A cross between a heterozygous single and a double should give equal numbers of singles and doubles (Ackerman and Williams 1982).

White flower color in Japanese iris is controlled by a single set of genes in which the nonwhite character (all colors other than white) is dominant and white is recessive. Apparently, this gene for white acts quite independently from the genes which control the various nonwhite colors (purples, violets, lavenders, etc.) and may be likened to an on-off switch. If one or both of the gene pair carries the factor for pigmented (nonwhite) flowers, then the resulting flower will be some color other than white. Only when neither gene pair carries the nonwhite color factor will the flower be white (Ackerman and Bentz 1986a).

Unfortunately, the patterns of inheritance among the various nonwhite flower pigments is highly complex. Detailed studies of large populations have shed but limited light on the subject.

This is perhaps why it has been so difficult to obtain pure blue, pink, or red flowers. These colors are invariably contaminated with traces of lavender or purple. If it were a simple case of a dominant-recessive relationship between the genes for these pigments (as is the case with nonwhite versus white flowers), then a hybridizer would merely need to make a series of crosses between two parents of a close approach to the desired pure color (or to self one parent) and grow out large populations. Theoretically, he could then expect to get one pure-colored flowering plant in every four, sixteen, or sixty-four seedlings, depending on whether there were one, two, or three sets of genes involved.

Following this procedure and involving very large populations has proved unsuccessful in obtaining the desired results. This suggests that there is a strong linkage between the genes controlling these flower pigments. Instead of being transmitted independently, they are inherited as units. Linkage is only rarely complete and may have been broken in the case of inheritance of pure pink flower color. This makes it probable that the linkage groups involving blue flower color may also be broken by the hybridizer of Japanese irises who has the patience and persistence to grow large populations from properly selected crosses (Ackerman and Bentz 1986b).

CHAPTER 10   *Handling Seeds and Seedlings*

Care and Planting of Seeds

PODS ARE HARVESTED when thoroughly mature. They are then brown and often beginning to crack open at the top. Care must be taken that they are not allowed to remain on the plants long enough to start spilling seeds. If it is necessary to leave a pod at a time when it might open before it can be harvested it can be covered with a piece of nylon stocking or fine cheesecloth tied at the bottom around the stalk below the pod. It is, of course, best to allow the pod to ripen fully on the plant. However, some seeds will mature in the case of pods accidentally broken off even when they are still partly green. If part of the stalk has broken off with the pod it can be placed in water changed daily. However if the bit of stalk is so short that the base of the pod might be in water it is wiser merely to allow the pod to continue ripening in the dry state lest it become moldy.

Planting Outdoors

Most commonly seeds are planted out of doors, although an alternative method is to start them indoors. Nature has devised a means of protecting sprouted seedlings from winter damage through an inhibiter in the skin of the seed which delays germination. This inhibiter is inactivated by a period of near-freezing temperature. In the north, where seeds sprouting in the late fall might not survive the winter, the inhibiter delays germination until it is inactivated by the cold and the seeds germinate in the spring. In warm regions seeds can be planted outdoors right after harvest and those that sprout in the fall as the inhibiter gradually wears off will probably suffer no winter damage in such mild climates. In the north, however, it is best to wait until late September or October to make sure germination will not occur until spring. In warm regions, if one wishes to speed up germination, the seeds can be kept in the refrigerator at a little above freezing (34–40° F) for a few weeks to hasten inactivation of the inhibiter (McEwen 1973, 1974; Bauer 1986).

Seeds can be planted directly in a prepared bed, but it is preferable to start them in flats or pots. As planting medium any good commercial germinating mix will serve, or one can be made with equal parts of finely ground sphagnum moss, vermiculite and sand. Some growers use a base of good sifted garden soil covered with an inch of clean sand, preferably sand that has been sterilized by an hour or more in the oven at 300° F. The sand protects the newly germinated seedlings from fungal infections such as damping off and the growing roots soon reach the soil. Meanwhile the seedlings are nourished for the first two or three weeks by their endosperm and subsequently, after they are an inch or so tall, they can be given feedings of acid-type fertilizer every ten days or so with their regular watering. Seeds are planted about ½ inch deep. In the pots they can be scattered over the surface about an inch apart and then covered with the selected growing mix or sand. In that way, the seeds of a single cross can be started in one labeled pot. In flats it is usual to plant the seeds about an inch apart in rows 2 or 3 inches apart with a suitable marker for each cross. Pots or flats can be placed in a cold frame or sheltered spot and, on the arrival of freezing weather, covered with a mulch to protect the seeds from being heaved and mixed. Even though the various crosses are identified with markers, it is wise to keep also a plan of the planting in case markers are lost or misplaced in removing the mulch in the spring. In the spring, covering the cold frame with its glass cover will help speed up germination.

Planting Indoors

Planting indoors under lights offers the advantage, especially in colder areas, of gaining an earlier start of two to four or more months which, in turn, makes it possible, under suitable conditions, to have bloom on most of one's seedlings the second year after planting and thus save a year (McEwen 1971b, Coble 1987a). If one has plenty of room or only a few seeds, the start can be made any time after the required period of moist-chill treatment described below, and growing plants can be successively moved into larger pots as needed. If one's space under lights is too limited to accommodate such larger pots, it is best to start no earlier than February, to avoid the need for transplanting until time to move out of doors.

Since indoor planting will not take place for some time after harvest, the seeds must be stored for that period, and the conditions under which they are stored control how successful subsequent germination will be. The essential conditions are three: (1) the seeds must have a period of exposure to cold, (2) they must be stored in the moist state, and (3) they must be healthy and free of infection (McEwen 1973, 1974; Bauer 1986).

The need for cold treatment has been explained above in the discussion of planting out of doors. Three weeks at a temperature of 34 to 40°F is probably adequate but a month or more is better, or the seeds can remain in the refrigerator for storage purposes if desired until the time for planting arrives. Care must be taken that the temperature does not go below freezing, as prolonged storage in the frozen state can be lethal to seeds (although not to pollen). The importance of the period of cold storage was quite dramatically shown in one experiment (McEwen 1973) in which only 16% of seeds stored at temperatures of 55 to 70% F germinated when subsequently planted and took an average of thirty days to do so, compared with 82% germination in fifteen days for seeds stored at 35 to 37°F.

The second condition is that the seeds be kept moist. This is readily done by placing them with a small amount of water in plastic packets. Sandwich bags serve well and unless the number of seeds is very large two packets can be made from each bag using the two bottom corners. If the seeds are stored directly after harvest while they still have some natural moisture, only a drop or two of water need be added to the packet of seeds before it is sealed and its label attached. Usually, however, seeds are left in their pods for some time before being removed and stored, and become quite dry. Depending on the dryness and the number of seeds in a packet, a few drops to a teaspoonful of water may be appropriate to make the seeds moist but not sloppily wet. Tap water appears to serve as well as sterile water. The packet must be carefully closed so that the moisture remains. The importance of storage in the moist state was also strikingly shown in the experiment cited above. Only 1.8% of seeds stored in the dry state germinated and the few that did required an average of twenty-one days, compared with 53% in four to seven days for seeds stored in packets with a few drops of water. These figures for the number of days for germination to occur were based on direct observation of seeds placed on moist filter paper in Petri dishes. More than four days elapse, of course, before seeds planted in flats show green sprouts breaking through the surface of the growing mix.

The third essential condition is to avoid infection. Dusting the seeds lightly with a protective fungicide such as thiram helps prevent fungal infection during storage. Also it is important to discard any nonviable seeds in the batch. Healthy, viable seeds have strong resistance to infection, but if they are nonviable they are very prone to infection and decay, and the bad seeds can spread the infection to good ones. Most nonviable seeds are easily distinguished by an obvious lack of the firm seed inside the outer covering.

The seeds can be planted in pots or ordinary flats as in the case of outdoor planting, but flats with individual compartments are preferable. They require more space than ordinary flats but permit a single seed to be planted in each compartment. When the seeds are started early they will be in the flats for a number of months and in ordinary flats or pots the roots become so intertwined that they suffer considerable damage when they are separated for transplanting in the garden. With the divided flats a single seed can be planted in each compartment and at transplanting time the seedling with its moistened ball of growing mix can be carefully lifted out and planted with very little disturbance of the roots.

About two weeks after the seed has sprouted (a few days after the green tip shows above the surface) its endosperm will be exhausted and it will then be dependent on nutrients in the growing medium for its nourishment. These are easily provided by adding every ten days or so some acid type soluble fertilizer to the regular schedule of watering. If the growing medium contains soil, fertilizing can be postponed until the leaves are 2 or 3 inches tall, but if an artificial mix has been used it should be started as soon as the sprout is seen. If one has a large number of flats, watering them in the space under their lights can be difficult and time consuming. An easy way to resolve this is to have shallow metal or plastic trays made about 1½ inches deep and large enough to hold a number of flats. Water (or dissolved fertilizer) poured into the trays waters the seedlings from below through the holes in the bottom of the flats and the excess water can be drained off when finished.

If one has a greenhouse it can, of course, be used for starting the seeds but that is not necessary. For only a few seeds a position in a sunny window in a warm room will do, with the flats turned each day to prevent the seedlings from leaning too far toward the light. With large numbers of flats, growing the seedlings under fluorescent lights gives superior results (McEwen 1971b). For this purpose pairs of one of the horticultural lights made for this purpose can be used, or results at least as good can be had with a combination of ordinary fluorescent lights, using in each pair one tube of cool white and one of warm white (daylight). Supplementing these with several low-wattage incandescent bulbs will add light from the lower (red) end of the spectrum needed for good plant growth but this is not essential. It is convenient to have the lights controlled by a timer set to have the lights on sixteen hours daily, or they can be left on constantly. Japanese irises appear to belong in that large group with seeds that germinate in either light or darkness but perhaps somewhat better in light (McEwen 1973). Probably, therefore, it is worthwhile to start the lights as soon as the seeds are planted instead of waiting until the green sprouts begin to appear above the surface. It is convenient to have the lights suspended from pulleys by ropes to make it easy to raise them as the little seedlings grow and keep the lights always safely above the tips of the leaves. The temperature of the room should be kept at 70 to 76° F until germination has occurred and then can be reduced to 60 to 70° F.

Lining Out

Seedlings are ready to be lined out in the garden as soon as they are 2 to 4 inches tall, although in very light soil it may be safer to wait until they are larger. If left too long in the small compartments of the divided flats they become root bound and deteriorate; therefore, if it is not possible to plant them in the garden when they have reached correct size they should be transplanted into larger pots. Before actual planting out of doors the seedlings should be gradually hardened by moving them from their warm sheltered environment for an increasing number of hours outside on warm days, or they can be moved to a cold frame, and its cover removed for gradually longer periods on good days. If the flats are watered prior to the planting to hold the mix together and the seedlings are lifted carefully, they are set back very little. A small kitchen fork makes an excellent tool for this purpose. Some flats have holes in the bottom of each compartment large enough to permit pushing the plants up without the use of a fork, and this causes even less disturbances to the roots. Since the seedlings will probably remain in place for three or more years they should be spaced at least 9 inches apart, and if space permits 12 inches is better. The bed should be well dug and raked before planting. In each small hole made to receive a seedling a handful of moist growing mix forming a nest to receive the small plant helps it become adjusted to its new home. The seedling is then watered with plain water or a weak solution (one-half usual strength) of soluble fertilizer of acid type. Subsequent watering with full strength soluble fertilizer several times, starting a few weeks after planting and after the usual time of Japanese iris bloom in addition to the regular schedule of granular fertilizer enhances growth that first year.

More than half of seedlings started under lights in February and cared for as described can be expected to bloom the second year, other circumstances being favorable. If an earlier start can be made still more will bloom the second year. If any have not bloomed by the third year they probably are not worth keeping unless from a cross of particular interest to the breeder.

CHAPTER 11   🌿   *Judging and Evaluation of Seedlings and Awards*

J UDGING OF Japanese irises—and other flowers—in the United States is of two general types: garden judging and show judging. Garden judging is the appraisal of plants as they are growing to select the best ones in various categories in accordance with standards set by the Society for Japanese Irises and the American Iris Society. Show judging is concerned with the quality of specimens displayed at shows.

Garden Judging

Garden judging and evaluation of seedlings are conveniently considered together because they have much in common. The official rules governing judging are discussed in detail in the American Iris Society's *Handbook for Judges and Show Officials* (1985). Welsh has discussed these rules as they apply to Japanese irises in a more recent excellent article that judges wishing up-to-date information will find helpful (Welsh 1988). In view of those detailed discussions of judging, only general principles need be considered here.

The standards set by rules of judging are essential to provide guidelines for the evaluation of flowers, but if too rigid they can lead hybridizers to work toward a common type, at least as regards form, with the result that desirable variations in form tend to be lost. Fortunately the early hybridizers of Japanese irises in the United States encouraged diversity of form (Payne 1964) and this point of view has continued and, indeed, grown stronger. The Society for Japanese Irises accepts all flower types—singles, doubles and multipetaled—as equally desirable. Within these types falls may be pendent, vertically arched, semiflaring, or horizontally flaring, with form open or compact, and standards may be of various sizes and positions, provided the total appearance is one of balance and grace. The flowers must also have the normal number of segments, in multiples of three, although this is not strictly required in the case of the style arms of doubles and the inner petals and petaloids of multipetaled flowers.

Pendent falls that hang limply cannot be attractive but those that arch downward in a graceful curve can be charming as seen in plates 6, 15, 16, and 25. Flowers of the single type usually reveal spaces between the falls. This is not a detriment unless the spaces are wider than the falls, making the blossom spindly. There are now also many single flowers with wide, round falls that overlap (figure 2, plates 7 and 21). This is a most attractive form but it would be a misfortune if all were bred to be like that. In the case of the double flowers a round, compact, flaring form with all petals overlapping is preferred by most. Small spaces between the falls toward the center of the flower are acceptable but large ones are not, by modern standards. A characteristic of many cultivars is increase in size of the flower from day one to day three. In such flowers small spaces that are acceptable on the day of opening may become unattractively large by the second day with the lengthening of the hafts. Another characteristic of many double Japanese irises is a tendency for the three inner petals to remain partly upright the first day. If the total effect in the clump, with some flowers fully open and others with three petals more or less upright, is not unattractive this should not be considered a fault provided all falls are in correct position by the second day. As has been noted above many Japanese iris blossoms increase in size from day one to day three. This is natural and desirable. Other cultivars have flowers which are of essentially the same size throughout the life of the blossom and this is normal for them and, of course, not a fault.

Another feature of double Japanese irises that demands comment is the comparative size of the three falls of the outer row and those of the inner row. Ideally, they should be the same size but usually the inner ones are smaller. In fact, a flower with all six of the same size is so rare that this feature cannot be too strictly judged. A blossom with all falls the same size deserves special commendation, other features being good also, but unless the difference in size is so great that the flower lacks balance, it should not be considered a significant fault.

Branches are an asset, but only if so placed that they and the blossoms they carry do not interfere with one another. It must be remembered also that the principal value of branching is to increase the bud count and thus prolong the period of bloom. Hence, a plant with no branch and only two or three buds at the terminal, but which sends up successive stalks can be better than one with branches of poor type. Unfortunately the judge usually sees the particular cultivar only once on a judging tour and hence cannot observe the plant's capacity to repeat. In the case of continuing bloomers, however, the newly appearing stalks can be seen and should be looked for.

In the past it was generally accepted that it was a fault for more than one blossom to be open on a stalk at a time. In a cultivar with only a few buds per bloomstalk this certainly is so, as it seriously shortens the period of bloom. Indeed, it would perhaps be ideal even in a cultivar with eight buds per stalk since it would ensure a bloom period of some twenty-four days. In modern varieties, however, with multiple buds per stalks, some overlap of bloom is inevitable and is not a fault. On the other hand it should not be given extra credit.

Colors should be clear and bright; flowers closer to true blue, red, or pink than any previously available deserve particular consideration. In many cultivars the color becomes somewhat lighter from day one to day three. If this is not unattractive it is not a fault. All patterns are desirable. In flowers with the lined type of patterns the lines that are sharply outlined are considered best, and branching of the lines, especially toward their ends, is desirable but its lack is not a fault.

The total clump effect depends greatly on leaves and stalks. Leaves must be of healthy green appearance and upright or gracefully arched at their tops. Plants with leaves that tend to sprawl as the season advances deserve no place in the garden and cannot be accepted no matter how good they may be in other respects. Stalks should be of a height to hold the flowers above the leaves. Flowers that seem to float just above the leaves are very attractive as also are those held well above, so long as the difference between the height of the leaves and of the stalks is not so great as to make the effect out of balance. Similarly, stalk height and flower size must be in balance. In the case of the miniatures the desirable ratio of flower diameter to stalk height is generally accepted to be roughly one to five, but this is not applicable to the large cultivars. In them, for example, a 10-inch flower can look in correct balance on a 36-inch stalk. If the usual ratio accepted for the miniature were demanded, a 12-inch blossom would require a stalk 60-inches tall. There could be few gardens where such a cultivar would be appropriate. What is of chief importance is the overall appearance of grace and balance in the clump.

A feature of particular importance is the strength of the stem between ovary and branch and of the perianth tube between ovary and blossom. These must be strong enough to hold the blossom in normal, upright position. This does indeed require strength because the large flowers are heavy, especially when the weight of rain is added. No matter how beautiful a Japanese iris may be it cannot be approved if it cannot hold up its head. Poor durability is also a major fault. A flower that lasts fewer days than is normal or that is spoiled by heat or a light rain easily borne by others cannot be approved.

Novelty, that is, the appearance of special features such as new colors, patterns, and forms, velvety texture, tetraploidy, and hybrids from wide crosses, is of great importance, and hybridizers working towards such new developments should be encouraged. Nevertheless Japanese irises presenting these features cannot be considered for higher awards unless they also meet other judging standards.

In closing this discussion of judging, let us return to the aspect of it with which the chapter began, the importance of not permitting our judging standards to become so specific that desirable types of flowers may gradually be lost. In Japan this is guarded against by the interest of various groups and breeders in particular types: Higos, Ises, and, perhaps to a lesser extent, Edos. In western countries those types, traditionally distinct in Japan, do not have their partisan adherents. Unquestionably, the large, ruffled Higos with their wide, overlapping falls are the ones that catch the attention and are preferred by most viewers, whether judges, breeders, or general garden visitors. This inevitably results in cultivars of that type being selected preferentially for hybridizing. The Society for Japanese Irises regards all types and all forms as equally desirable so long as they have beauty, balance, and grace. Nevertheless, a strong commitment by hybridizers is needed if breeding programs are to continue to produce new and improved examples of the charming Ise type and the more open character of the older Edos.

Evaluation of Seedlings

In evaluating seedlings the hybridizer naturally has in mind the features of importance to the judge. If he is evaluating one as a possible candidate for registration his standards must be no less strict than those of the judge. When, however, he is appraising them as potentially important in his breeding program he can place greatest weight on the presence of special features that offer promise toward his goals. Nevertheless, it is essential in making these selections not to choose plants that obviously carry genes for serious faults.

Awards

The awards of the American Iris Society are of a number of types: garden awards, convention awards, and show awards. Garden awards include those of High Commendation (HC), Regional Test Garden Awards (RTG), Honorable Mention (HM), Award of Merit (AM), and, the highest of all, the Dykes Memorial Medal. According to the rules of the American Iris Society all types of irises are eligible for the Dykes Memorial Medal but in the United States it has been awarded to date only to bearded irises.

Only bearded irises are eligible for the Award of Merit but there are equivalent ones for other irises. In the case of Japanese irises this is the Payne Award, named in honor of Arlie Payne. The Payne winners and their hybridizers for each year since 1966 when the award began are as follows:

Payne Award Winners

1966 Strut and Flourish (Payne)	1978 Tuptim (Rich)
1967 Leave Me Sighing (Maddocks)	1979 Prairie Velvet (Hazzard)
1968 Dancing Waves (Payne)	1980 Purple Parasol (McEwen)
1969 Star at Midnight (Rich)	1981 Fuji (Abell)
1970 Worley Pink (Worley)	1982 Returning Tide (McEwen)
1971 Numazu (Hazzard)	1983 Raspberry Rimmed (McEwen)
1972 no award	1984 no award
1973 Hue and Cry (Maddocks)	1985 Blue Marlin (Copeland)
1974 no award	1986 Ipsus (Innerst)
1975 Prairie Love Song (Hazzard)	1987 Freckled Geisha (Reid)
1976 Stranger in Paradise (Hager)	1988 Oriental Eyes (Vogt)
1977 no award	1989 Blueberry Rimmed (McEwen)

TABLE 2. *Rules Governing Japanese Iris Awards*

	Eligibility	Votes Required	Number of Irises a Judge May Vote for	Years Eligible and Permitted on Ballot
Garden Awards				
High Commendation (HC)	New seedling not yet introduced	5	3	Unlimited until introduction
Honorable Mention (HM)	2d year after introduction	10	3	Eligibility unlimited. On ballot only 4 years
Payne Award	2nd through 5th year after HM	Highest number of votes; minimum of 10	1	4
Dykes Medal	2nd through 4th year after Payne award	15% of votes cast	1	3
Show Awards				
Exhibition Certificate	Entered officially at an approved show	5	Unlimited	NA
Convention Awards				
Franklin Cook Cup	Originated and introduced outside host region and seen on garden tours	Largest number of votes cast by all convention attendees (not limited to judges)	1	NA
President's Cup	Originated and introduced within host region and seen on tours	Same as above	1	NA

Convention Awards, which include the Franklin Cook Cup and the President's Cup, are given to irises seen and voted on in the tour gardens at AIS conventions each year. Since Japanese irises are not in bloom at that convention time, it is improbable that they will be contenders for these awards, although they are eligible. However, comparable awards are voted at the conventions of the Society for Japanese Irises.

Show Awards are given to irises seen at shows. The rules regarding them are the same as those for other flowers. Most shows today are judged on the cultivar basis, that is, each named cultivar is judged not in terms of its comparison with other cultivars at the show but on the basis of its quality compared with that particular cultivar in general. Not the plant, but the ability of the person who brought it as a grower and exhibitor is being judged. One feature that differs from what is usually admired in show judging requires comment, namely the presence of more than one open blossom on a stalk. In the case of Japanese irises this should not be counted an asset. If the specimen in question has branches with six or more buds and that cultivar normally opens more than one blossom per scape at one time, this should not be considered a fault. If, however, the specimen has only a few buds and two are open it is a fault for it is not only undesirable but it is also most improbable that such a cultivar could normally have more than one blossom open at a time.

In contrast to show bench judging of named cultivars, judging of seedlings at a show is similar to that of garden judging.

The rules governing the granting of awards for which Japanese irises are eligible are summarized in Table 2 (p. 103).

CHAPTER 12 ☙※❧ *Registration and Introduction*

Registration

B EFORE 1920 there was no provision for registering an iris. Cultivars were named by growers and listed for sale but there was no official recognition of that name nor assurance that two plants with that name were actually the same. The inauguration by the American Iris Society in 1920 of an official registry of irises, including Japanese irises, was extremely important. Today it is essential that anyone wishing to give a name to a seedling take the necessary steps to register it. Registration provides a record of information about the cultivar and ensures that its name can refer only to it. In Japan there is no official registering agency and plants are merely named, listed, and offered for sale by the breeders (Hirao 1987). Some originating in Japan now, however, are being registered for their hybridizers with the American Iris Society. Hybridizers of all countries may make use of the registration services of the American Iris Society. In Australia, Germany, Great Britain, and New Zealand this is done through the registrar of the national iris society who then coordinates the registration with the registrar of the American Iris Society.

The total number of Japanese irises registered by the American Iris Society is small compared to that of tall bearded irises. Nevertheless, the number increases annually and the hybridizer should consider carefully whether the cultivar in question is sufficiently different from or better than ones already in commerce to warrant adding to the number. It is well to observe the plant in bloom for at least two years before making a decision about it, as seedlings may not be typical in their first year of bloom. Also it is seldom advisable to register a plant unless it probably will be subsequently introduced, as otherwise it encumbers the checklist with plants that are unobtainable.

How to Register

The registrar, whose name and address are shown in the *Bulletin of the American Iris Society,* can provide all necessary information as well as the official forms needed for registration. A first step is to select a name not previously used for any iris and in accordance with the rules established by the International Horticultural Code. These are printed on the reverse of the registration form and, together with detailed instructions regarding registration and introduction, are published periodically in the *Bulletin of the American Iris Society* (Nelson 1989).

Introduction

Introduction is the offering of a plant for sale to the public through catalogs, lists, or advertisements. An advertisement in the *Bulletin of the American Iris Society* automatically records the plant as introduced, but any other advertisements or types of notice must be sent by first class mail to the registrar who will return to the introducer official notice that the introduction has been recorded. An iris is not eligible for awards higher than that of High Commendation until it has been introduced. The hybridizer should take even greater pains in evaluating a plant for introduction than for registration and should not offer it for sale until there is enough stock to meet anticipated orders.

Increasing Stock

The decision to introduce a plant often presents the hybridizer with the dilemma of needing to accumulate stock of it as rapidly as possible and yet wishing to use it as a parent for crosses. One method of solving the problem is to divide the plant as it is growing in the garden by means of two spading forks inserted in the clump back to back. In this way one piece is available for crossing and the other can be divided into one or two rhizome divisions and lined out. Increasing stock as rapidly as possible is particularly important also to enable the serious hybridizer to send his new seedlings to conventions and other gardens where they can be seen and judged. Even the most beautiful new flower can receive no recognition if it is "born to blush unseen."

CHAPTER 13 ⚜ *The*
Japanese Iris Show

ONE OF THE BEST WAYS to introduce the general public to the beauty of Japanese irises is by holding a Japanese iris show. The first known Japanese iris show in the United States was staged at Kalamazoo, Michigan, on July 6, 1963 by the Southwestern Michigan Iris Society. This was repeated in 1964, 1968, and again in 1977, after which it became an annual event. Since then, shows for Japanese irises have been held in several locations, some of them, for instance, in Summerville, South Carolina, becoming annual events. At least seven such shows were known to be held in 1988.

In choosing the time for an all-Japanese iris show the date should be set for expected peak bloom. In areas where other late irises somewhat overlap in bloom time with the Japanese it may be preferable to have a late iris show, setting the date so as to catch some bloom of several types. These are usually billed as beardless iris shows since most late-blooming irises are beardless types. When it becomes a choice between a slightly early or slightly late date for an area, the earlier date is probably preferable. If the season is late, there will likely be other irises in bloom on the earlier date, but if the season is early all may be gone by the later date. American Iris Society rules should be followed for an accredited show.

Usually, the Japanese iris show is small compared to tall bearded shows, but it makes up for its lack of size through novelty and beauty. It is of considerable help to include an artistic arrangement division. Flower arrangers especially enjoy working with the Japanese iris, and with a little effort in publicity a good number of garden-club members may enter the competition. If any growers in the area have sufficient quantities of Japanese irises it is advisable to make blooms available for use by arrangers who may not have them in their own gardens. The schedule of arrangement classes to be shown may be as diverse and interpretive as is appropriate for the level of arrangers' skills in the particular area, but it is a good idea to encourage the use of, or at least to include, some classes to be done in the Japanese manner of arranging. Using the Japanese manner of arranging (Wong 1987) is not only natural for Japanese irises, but usually requires fewer blooms than the more massive arrangements of the western style. Modern or contemporary line arrangements also work very well.

If there is an Ikebana group in the area, or one of the schools of Japanese arranging such as a Sogetsu school, it is especially helpful if they will stage an exhibition in conjunction with the show. This adds both size and interest, and the two displays are by nature compatible. The number of flowers required and the versatility usually desired by the exhibiting group means that many flowers other than irises will probably be used, but a few Japanese iris blooms should be made available to the group for use. This helps to create unity in the overall display and further emphasizes possible uses of Japanese irises. Interest may be heightened if one or more of the Ikebana members can give demonstrations in flower arranging at specified times during the day.

In staging and judging the horticultural specimens, it is necessary to keep in mind a few points unique to this type of show. Since most Japanese irises are fairly long stemmed, and the bloom faces upward, the show should be staged on low tables, benches, or ledges. It is disconcerting to the viewers and the judges to be looking up at the underside of a tall-stemmed bloom staged on a table of normal height. It may be possible to cut some stem off, but this affects proportion. Since it is normal for some to grow tall, and judging should be based on how well the iris is grown for its variety, cutting much off the stem is usually not desirable. Containers should be of sufficient height and size to work well with the iris. The diameter of the container opening should not be too large, as stems are slender, and a large opening needs too much wedging to hold the stems firmly vertical.

Japanese irises naturally look attractive near water. If the show is in a shopping mall or other facility where a pool or fountain is part of the decor, it can often be used to advantage as a backdrop for at least part of the display.

Another idea sometimes used for increasing the size and interest of a show is to include a division for companion plants—those which bloom at the same time as Japanese irises and will look attractive with them in perennial plantings. Also included may be background or groundcover plants.

It is important to have judges who are familiar with Japanese irises. In judging the Japanese iris it should be remembered that after opening they are constantly changing. On the second day the color will often be a little lighter than when first opened, the size will usually have increased, and sometimes form will change noticeably. If condition and substance is still good, the second- and third-day flower is to be considered just as typical, and as good a specimen, as the first-day bloom. It is desirable to stage the show as a "cultivar show," as most other iris shows are now done. This means that each variety is judged as a separate class and is judged according to a standard of perfection for that particular variety.

It is helpful to include a sale of Japanese irises at the time of the show as visitors inevitably wish to obtain some for their own gardens. To this end it is useful also to have available at the reception desk a list and, if possible, catalogs of sources where Japanese irises can be obtained as well as simple printed sheets outlining the basic culture of these flowers. Unquestionably, a show helps greatly to stimulate local interest in Japanese irises.

ᨓ *Around the World*

Chapters 1 and 2 give historical accounts of Japanese irises in Japan and the United States. This appendix details organizational activities in those two countries and presents the meager information we have been able to obtain about interests in Japanese irises in some other countries through personal conversations and letters. Such information as we have is, indeed, so inadequate that we hesitate to present it but do so on the principle that this little may be better than none, and, especially, in the hope that it may stimulate interest and encourage growers of Japanese irises around the world to provide more adequate information.

Argentina

Our knowledge about Japanese irises in South America is especially limited with information only for Argentina and Chile. Monica Pool of Buenos Aires reports that there are always people interested in growing irises locally but as yet no garden society is devoted to them. As in most countries interest is chiefly in tall bearded irises but she and Domingo Petraroia of the Argentina Horticultural Faculty are particularly interested in Siberian and Japanese irises and have done some hybridizing with them. The influence of Walter Marx reached even to Argentina, for Monica Pool first became interested in Japanese irises in 1955 through one of his colorful advertisements.

Severe heat in midsummer makes it difficult to grow Japanese irises in the garden and she has found it much better to grow them in pots in a pool. At first she tried removing the pots from the pool during the winter months but they did poorly and she now leaves them in the pool all winter, repotting them as they become too large. Having the pots stand in water all winter is in striking contrast to the need to remove them and bury them in soil under a protective mulch in colder regions.

Since Argentina is in the southern hemisphere, peak bloom in the region of Buenos Aires is late October for the tall bearded irises and mid-November for the Japanese.

Australia

The Iris Society of Australia is a very active organization with many enthusiastic members. There is no group concerned specifically with Japanese irises but a good many individual members grow them. The New South Wales Region has a mini-show for them at their December meeting and the Hemerocallis Society has a Japanese iris display at their December meeting. Gordon Loveridge, of Leura, estimates that, in general, they rank second to tall bearded irises in popularity although in the region of Sydney probably in third place after Louisianas.

Northern Victoria is rather too warm for Japanese irises but they do well in the cooler, hilly areas around Melbourne. They succeed also in the coastal regions of New South Wales and in the hills around Adelaide in South Australia, and probably best in Tasmania where the cooler climate suits them. In Western Australia they succeed only in the southeast corner around Perth, and in Queensland only in the south coastal section, although even there it is subtropical and rather warm for them. The soil is acid along the coast but alkaline inland where it is also dry and hot making conditions unsuitable (Blyth 1988, Loveridge 1988). They bloom in late November and December when hot, northerly winds are frequent. Hence, in the Melbourne area it is recommended that they be grown in pots which can be moved to a shady, protected place when necessary; and for those planted in the ground a site with filtered shade is advisable (Tilley 1988). Myrtle Murray of Brookvale in New South Wales also grows them in pots. She has grown Japanese irises since 1976 with success and hybridizes them but has not yet introduced any. Graeme Grosvenor of Rainbow Ridge Nurseries, near Sidney and Gordon Loveridge, whose nursery is in Leura, also hybridize with the aim of developing improved cultivars for introduction.

The Australian government's import regulations require that plants coming into the country spend a period in quarantine, during which they are subject to methyl bromide fumigation. This presents some difficulty in obtaining new varieties from other countries but Graeme Grosvenor and Gordon Loveridge have been able to obtain them; and Barry Blyth of Temp Two Nursery, after giving up Japanese irises for a time some years ago, has imported some one hundred varieties from Japan and the United States since 1983.

The opposite seasons north and south of the equator pose a question of timing for growers in the United States and Japan who wish to ship plants to Australia. Loveridge believes that shipping in September and October is best. Roots are inevitably damaged by the methyl bromide fumigation and if this injury occurs in April and May in the Australian winter the roots have little opportunity to recover if planted out of doors. When that damage occurs in September, in the Australian spring, the roots are stimulated to regrow. This is, of course, less of an issue if the plants are to be started in pots in a greenhouse.

Belgium and the Netherlands

Belgium has the distinction of being the first western country to be introduced to Japanese irises. Between 1820 and 1830, Philipp Franz von Siebold, a German physician serving with the Netherlands army in the Dutch East Indies, spent much time in Japan on a mission there and was able to indulge his special interest in studying and collecting native plants. Shortly after Japan was opened to foreign trade by Admiral Perry in 1853, von Siebold returned to Japan, established a nursery there and in 1857 sent Japanese irises to Belgium where they were grown in the Vershaffelt Nursery in Ghent. These were probably the first Japanese irises to be grown and distributed in Europe. Subsequently, he established his own nursery in Leyden. He introduced a number of Japanese irises including "Alexandre von Humboldt," a white single; "Professor de Vreise," a single with darker veins on lighter lavender falls; "Alexandre von Sieboldt," a rich reddish-purple single; and "Souvenir," a lovely single pink. Louis Benoit Van Houtte (1810–76), a famous Belgian commercial nurseryman and editor of the Belgian horticultural magazine *Flore de serres et des jardins de l'Europe,* using von Siebold's plants and probably others imported from Japan undertook an extensive hybridizing program. Von Siebold's four irises mentioned above and fifteen of Van Houtte's own introductions, which are shown in color in volumes 20 (1874) and 23 (1880) of the *Flore de serres,* illustrate well Hirao's comment, quoted in chapter 1, that during the time of Matsudaira Shōō (who died in 1856) all the types, colors, and patterns seen in modern hybrids had already been achieved.

Today there are individuals interested in various types of irises but no garden society devoted to them. Alphonse Van Mulders reports that in 1943 he worked in the famous nursery of Jules Buyssens in Uccle where at that time there were thirty-nine varieties of Japanese irises. In 1948 he took the best of these to the Jardenart-Van Mulders at Wijgmaal/Leuven and has since then added newer ones.

An important new venture is that of Koen Engelen of Ranst, who in 1987 started an iris nursery and has accumulated a fine collection of Japanese irises which he expects to have commercially available by 1990. He reports that they grow well there both in pots and in garden beds, apparently finding the mild, moist, and misty coastal climate to their liking.

In Holland the situation is similar. The great firms known internationally to the bulb trade grow thousands of bulbous irises. As noted above von Sieboldt established a nursery specializing in Japanese irises in Leyden and the famous Ruys, Royal Moehrheim Nurseries in Dedemovaeert, listed Japanese and bearded irises as well as bulbous ones.

Today, K. Zahin, whose large nursery is in Alphen aan den Rijn has interest in Japanese irises and makes periodic trips to Japan.

Chile

I am indebted to Fred M. Schlegel of the University Austral Valdivia for the following information. He reports that cultivation of irises in Chile is almost entirely limited to older and a few more recent tall bearded cultivars. A few Japanese irises were brought to the Osorno and Llanquihue provinces of south-central Chile about 1930 by descendants of the German colonizers of the 1860s. Conditions there are good, with acid soil and mild climate. Rain is adequate from May to November but extra water may be needed during their summer in December through March.

In central Chile in the region of Santiago it is warmer, with hot dry summers that make pot culture in pools the best way to grow Japanese irises. Roman Wygnanki introduced them in that area about 1940, and in the 1960s the landscape architect Hans Lembcke used them in garden designs involving pools.

Since 1980 Schlegel has raised from seeds some fifteen cultivars of modern type in the Valdivia area of south-central Chile and is actively crossing them. He has started a Japanese and Siberian iris display along the banks of a river and is using them and Pacific Coast irises along small streams in parks, and at the Botanic Garden of the University Austral Valdivia.

Japanese irises in Chile start spring growth in August and bloom from late November to early January. Temperatures in winter may occasionally go a few degrees below freezing. A mulch is used primarily to maintain soil moisture. Schlegel knows of no problems as yet with diseases or insect pests.

England

Japanese irises must have been introduced to England within a few years of von Siebold's introduction of them in Belgium. Volume 23 of *Flore de serres et des jardins de l'Europe* (1888) shows pictures of two English cultivars, "Edward George Henderson" dated 1874 and "Sir Stafford Northcote" of 1880. The former is credited to Henderson and the latter to James Veitch whose nurseries in Exeter and Chelsea were famous for introducing to Europe many plants native to South America and other countries. A search at the Lindley Library of the Royal Horticultural Society by Anne Blanco White disclosed records of twenty-eight Japanese irises named by English breeders that were given First Class Certificates by the Royal Horticultural Society between 1874 and 1896. Veitch led with sixteen. Four others were named by the noted firm of Barr and Sons, three by George Gordon of Chelsea and one each by Bull, Henderson, Macleay, and Ware. All these highly regarded men had widely ranging interests in which Japanese irises played only a minor role. William Bull, whose nursery was also in Chelsea was interested in rare plants of all types, especially orchids. Sir George Macleay of Surry received honors for his horticultural achievements and was a Fellow of the Linnean Society. Thames Softley Ware of the Hale Farm Nurseries of Tottenham,

Middlesex, also named a number of bearded irises. Amos Perry of Middlesex, who introduced "Mount Hood" in 1889, continued for many years with eighteen or more varieties including "Mrs. Stanley," a rosy double, in 1925 and "Pandora," a light blue, in 1940. Kelways Nursery in Somerset is credited with "Shiski-Ikara," a very dark blue double in 1910. R. Wallace and Company of Colchester introduced a number in 1910, including "Deep Blue Waters," "Cloisonné" (a marbled double), "Distant Mountain," "Morning Mists," "Silver Stars," and "Peace," some of which may still be grown. In that period also the firm of V. N. Gauntlett and Co. of Chiddingfold, Surrey, listed some fifty or more Japanese irises and exported to the Continent and the United States.

After World War I growers of Japanese irises included Frank Lilly of the island of Guernsey and Maurice Prichard and Sons of Christchurch who in 1928 and 1929 introduced at least ten, including the famous "Mulberry," a double red, "Duchess of Abercorn," "Miss Goddard," "Peacock," "Rosy Morn," and "Sultan." P. S. Haward, of Clacton-on-Sea, not only raised Japanese irises but also wrote about them in gardening publications, as did that most famous irisarian of all, William Rickatson Dykes.

In more recent years individual members of the British Iris Society and general gardeners throughout the British Isles have grown Japanese irises and there are some at Wisley and fine plantings at Saville Garden at Windsor, but up to 1976 there was no organized effort. As in the United States, the British Iris Society's shows are scheduled for bloom of the bearded irises, so that the later blooming sorts are shown infrequently, and only recently has there been a purposeful effort to arouse interest in the beardless irises. This occurred in 1976 when the Siberian, Spuria, and Japanese Group was founded. The driving force behind it was Alex Back who recruited the interest of a number of founding members and the group was launched that June at an inaugural meeting attended by a dozen or so in the Royal Horticultural Society's New Hall. Jennifer Hewitt was elected Chairman with Doris Hansford Morris as Treasurer and Alex Back as Secretary. He, tragically, was struck by a car and killed only two months later, but his colleagues, very soon joined by Joan Trevithick as editor of the group's newsletter and as secretary-treasurer, and by others, carried on the new endeavor that he had inspired.

Starting with twenty members in 1976, the group had grown to seventy-five members in the British Isles and fifteen overseas by 1986. The group has an excellent relationship with the British Iris Society which helped it become organized, cooperates closely, and gives it coverage in its newsletter. Currently, the S. S. and J. Group, as its members refer to it, is growing in membership and stature. At its start most members were chiefly concerned with Siberian irises, with Spurias second, but interest in Japanese irises has grown in recent years. A number of commercial nurseries have joined the group, and plants and seeds are offered. Several members have particular interest in Japanese irises, notably, J. E. Venner, currently chairman of the group; Anne Blanco White, president of the British Iris Society, who serves as Japanese iris representative of the S. S. and J. Group; H. R. Jeffs, a past president of the British Irish Society; Norman Payne, a recent Japanese iris enthusiast; and Philip Allery who is actively hybridizing and has registered "Aldridge Parasol." Important aims of the group are the scheduling of shows and garden tours for Japanese and other late-blooming sorts, the development of trial plantings at the Royal Horticultural Society's gardens at Wisley and other properly cared-for public gardens throughout the country, encouraging commercial growers to offer good samplings of the best varieties, and the education of members in the culture of Japanese irises and the rewards of hybridizing them.

France

Doubtless, Japanese irises found their way into France within a few years of von Siebold's introduction of them in Belgium in 1857, but the earliest note that we have seen is that they were listed by Ragot Père, Fils et Gendre of Chatou (S&O) in 1893. The famous firm of Vilmorin, Andrieux et Cie of Paris established before 1745, began to specialize in irises by 1900 and introduced a number of bearded ones. They grew Japanese irises among others, and were one of the European firms that shipped to American nurseries in early days. The old firm of Tubat et Cie in Paris also provided Japanese irises and in 1926 introduced "Alsace-Lorraine," "Baron de Menars," "M. Abel Grottery," "Mlle. Blanche de Sommer," "Mme. Orny," and "Pierre Cochet."

The Societé d'Iris has some five hundred members whose interests are chiefly tall bearded irises, and there are no groups within the society with a particular concern for Japanese or other beardless types. Nevertheless, there are well-grown collections at the Parc de Bagatelle in Paris and in the botanical garden at Nantes, and there are sections for them at the large garden expositions such as those held periodically at Orleans.

The chief source today is the large nursery, Ets. Horticoles Cayeux, in Poilly-les-Gien about seventy-five miles due south of Paris. The nursery is concerned almost exclusively with irises, with many acres of tall beardeds and large numbers of some of the beardless ones also. Jean Cayeux started growing Japanese irises many years ago in his father's and grandfather's famous nursery near Paris with a few very old varieties including some of obviously French origin such as "La Candeur" and "Comtesse de Paris." Those were discarded when he bought twenty-five varieties from Walter Marx in 1959 and these came with him when he started his own iris nursery in Gien in 1960. Some Payne varieties and others from Japan and the United States were added, and he currently grows some sixty varieties and is adding to his list. The large perennial nursery Ets. Lepage of Angers also offers some Japanese irises.

Jean Cayeux reports that large areas of France are very well suited for growing Japanese irises including almost all the western section from Spain to Belgium and the central area where the soil also tends to be acid and there is abundant moisture.

Jean Peyrard, an amateur enthusiast in Seyssinet, has obtained seeds and has also imported fine modern varieties suitable for hybridizing with the ultimate goal of developing miniatures with long season of bloom. Jean Cayeux also has seedlings which will show their first bloom about 1990.

Germany

The German firm of L. Boehmer and Co. established a nursery in Yokahama in 1889–1901, one of the first foreign ones permitted in Japan. Boehmer exported chiefly to the nursery of Alfred Unger in Heidelberg-Schlierbach which, in turn, exported many to the United States.

No account of Japanese irises can fail to praise the work of Max Steiger of Laue near Nürnberg, who was one of the first to develop some tetraploid plants and is especially remembered today for his success in raising his care strain cultivars that tolerated alkaline conditions. The extraordinary insight of this remarkable man is well illustrated by his efforts to introduce yellow into the color range of Japanese irises by crosses with *I. pseudacorus* some fifteen years before this was achieved in Japan. His efforts did not succeed, but clearly he understood the possibilities and the genetic difficulties involved (Steiger 1960).

The former Deutsche Iris- und Liliengesellschaft has broadened its interests to embrace a wide variety of perennials changing its name to Gesellschaft der Staundenfreunde. Bearded irises are seen in many gardens but interest in Japanese irises has not been great in recent years. An excellent display of them in the International Garden Exposition in Hamburg in 1973 made an impression at the time. Such outstanding public plantings as the Palmengarten in Frankfurt have clumps growing beside streams and pools but not in large displays.

In recent years, Eckard Berlin in Biberach-an-der-Riss, has included Japanese irises in his very serious hybridizing program and has successfully used colchicine to convert them as well as Siberian irises and *I. pseudacorus* to the tetraploid state. Uwe Knöpnadel's Friesland Staudengarten in Jever, northern Germany, also has a collection of modern Japanese irises.

In East Germany the nursery of Eberhard Schuster of Augustenhof, which specializes in plants of "water garden" type, includes a selection of good varieties of Japanese iris as ones that grow well beside water.

Italy

In northern Italy in the region of the Alps, where the climate is suitable for Japanese irises, conditions are similar to those in Switzerland. As one moves south the climate becomes warmer and drier, and Margaret Cameron Longo, one of the very active members of the Società dell'Iris, doubts that

Japanese iris are grown south of Milan. The world-renowned iris garden in Florence managed and cared for by the society holds an annual international competition for bearded irises. Japanese irises are not included in the competition, but there is a planting of Arlie Payne's cultivars around a pool which was constructed for them.

Japan

In 1930 George M. Reed, Curator of Plant Pathology at the Brooklyn Botanic Garden and in charge of a special study of Japanese irises there, visited Japan under the auspices of the Botanic Garden and of the American Iris Socity. In Tokyo he was warmly welcomed and entertained by influential people interested in the *hanashōba*. In his discussion with his Japanese hosts the suggestion was made that an organization similar to the American Iris Society be founded. This was enthusiastically received and in a short time the Nihon Hanashōbu Kyokai was established. At the start the position of president was unfilled but Manobu Myoshi was vice president, and Kihei Ikeda executive secretary. After World War II, Kiyoshi Inoshita was elected president. He was succeeded by Jokichi Nambu and in 1975 by Shuichi Hirao who continued as president until his death in 1988.

The society's yearbook was first published in 1931 and has continued to the present. Meetings are held several times yearly in Tokyo and other cities with attendance of about one hundred participants. As its name implies the major interest is in Japanese irises with lesser concern for others. There are some six hundred members from all parts of the country including both amateur and commercial growers of Japanese irises. Members act as leaders in their districts with many visitors to the gardens each year. Some of the larger ones are visited by hundreds of thousands.

There is no agency for registering irises in Japan. Names are chosen by the breeder and are publicized in articles and at meetings. Over the years there has been some confusion of names, and some misnaming. The society attempts to correct such errors each year and distributes some authentically named cultivars to members.

In 1967, under the stimulus of Akira Horinaka, a second society was started with major interest in irises other than the hanashōbu. Horinaka, who has been its president since it was founded, reports that there are some one hundred members most of whom belong only to the one society. In Japanese the name of the older society is Nihon Hanashōbu Kyokai (Japan Hanashōbu Society) and that of the younger one Nihon Iris Kyokai but in the western world both, unfortunately, have been translated very similarly. The older society is called in English "The Japan Iris Society," and the newer one omits "The." Quite naturally, but regrettably, that slight difference usually is not noticed in western countries with the result that there is confusion as to identity. The difference, however, is real.

Throughout Japan there are over two hundred large plantings of Japanese irises, visited by some six million people each year. Mototeru Kamo and the late Shuichi Hirao have brought these large *hanashōbu* gardens into one organization, the name of which can be translated as Japanese Iris Garden Society (Kamo 1989).

New Zealand

We are indebted to Frances Love, president of the New Zealand Iris Society and to Heather Collins, Grant Iles, and Paul Richardson for such information as we have regarding Japanese irises in New Zealand. The society is an active one with members interested in all type of irises but with the bearded ones the most popular. The beardless irises, especially Siberians and spurias, are growing in popular interest and an increasing number of members are turning also to Japanese irises, usually referred to as Higos. Frances Love remarks that people are becoming "pool minded" in their gardening which furthers the planting of Japanese irises. She comments on plants she has seen that have shown a second period of bloom and cites a garden where the soil is moist all year, where Japanese irises that had bloomed normally in December and in late February showed "a mass of buds ready to bloom in March" (Love 1988).

Climatic conditions vary greatly from north to south, with the northern part of the North Island semitropical and the southern part of the South Island fairly cold in winter. A spine of mountains running from the middle of the North Island to the southern tip of the South Island also makes climatic differences, with good rainfall west of the mountains but drier conditions east of them. January and February are hot and dry, June and July cold and much less dry. Japanese irises grow well in the North Island, but are not much grown in the colder South Island. Soil pH varies from place to place. In most areas the natural degree of acidity suits Japanese irises well, but former pasture land that has been treated with lime might require correction.

Grant Iles, whose Bay Bloom Nursery is in Tauranga on the eastern mid-coast of the North Island, reports that Japanese irises grow very well there. He had previously had a problem with root knot nematodes but in the move from the previous site to Tauranga he believes he has controlled the infestation by treating the plants with Nemacur and planting them in sterilized beds. He knows of no other disease or pest problems.

The Bay Bloom Nursery has Japanese irises originally obtained from Japan and from Lorena Reid in Oregon. Grant Iles believes no one is actively hybridizing Japanese irises at present although both he and Phyllis Kokich have done so on a small scale in the past.

As in the United States, but in reverse order, season of bloom varies greatly from north to south starting in December in the north and progressing to March in the south. The position of the country below the equator raises the same question as in Australia regarding the best time to ship plants coming from the United States. On the basis of experience quoted by the late Jean Collins (1978) the preferred time is late September and October when the plants are preparing for dormancy in their American gardens but will be encouraged to start growth again on arrival in New Zealand's spring. Grant Iles states that plants imported from countries in the northern hemisphere are very slow in starting growth with some remaining dormant for nearly twelve months. Certainly this is due to the problem the plants face in adjusting to a new life cycle. Aside from this there are no difficulties in importing plants. There is no quarantine and merely the usual phytosanitery certificate required for all shipments of plants from one country to another certifying that the plants have been inspected by an authorized official in the garden of origin and found free of disease.

Switzerland

In Switzerland the soil, except for the Ticino Canton in the south, tends to be alkaline due to a rich content of calcium carbonate. As a result such alkaline intolerant plants as azaleas, rhododendrons, and Japanese irises are difficult to grow in some areas. There is no group within the Swiss Iris Society with particular interest in Japanese irises. Kazu Hisano of Ponte Cremenaga, the Botanical Garden of Geneva, and Thomas Bürge of Wabern, have collections of Japanese irises, and the latter has done some hybridizing on a small scale but, as yet, has named no seedlings.

Union of Soviet Socialist Republics

Plants of the wild *I. ensata* are extremely hardy and grow well and widely in the far eastern region of Siberia where they are natives. Not surprisingly, however, even the hardiest ones collected by N. V. Vereshchagina in the region of Gorno-Altaisk where temperatures fall to -49 F° did better, with larger plants and flowers, when grown under less harsh conditions (Rodionenko 1964)

The Russian botanist E. Regel tried growing cultivated hybrids in 1880 in what was then St. Petersburg but they did not survive. Professor Nosilov grew them in Moscow prior to World War II using special measures but subsequent attempts by the botanical garden there were discouraging. In contrast they grow well on the Black Sea coast and other areas where temperature and other environmental conditions are favorable. About 1926–27 thirty cultivated hybrids were brought from Japan to Sukhumi on the Black Sea for planting in the All-Union Institute of Horticulture. In 1930 more were imported, and by 1934 about one hundred varieties were well established and some were sent to other botanical gardens at Tbilisi and at Baku farther south on the Caspian Coast. The botanist and plant collector Vasily Alferov worked with the collection at Sukhumi but later it was moved to a State Farm at Adler fifty miles north on the Black Sea.

G. I. Rodionenko, Director of the Leningrad Botanical Garden, obtained a number of plants from Adler after World War II. Without good winter protection some were lost the first winter, and the others deteriorated over a period of two or three years; even with protection they grew poorly. His efforts therefore were directed toward obtaining hybrids hardy in Leningrad by crossing the cultivated varieties with native *I. ensata* collected in the northeast. In 1956 he obtained such a seedling, which he named after Vasily Alferov, from a cross of "Sano Watashi" by a native plant collected near Vladivostok. It is single and has the wine-red color of the species, with nicely arched form and wider falls (Rodionenko 1987).

By 1952 some twenty remaining cultivars at Adler were moved back to Sukhumi where they and a few new ones became the starting collection for the hybridizing efforts of Tatjana Chochua. Between 1962 and 1979 she grew some seven thousand seedlings of which fifty-five were selected for naming, including "Avtandil," "Amtekel," "Belaya Notch," and "Rica," all singles, and the doubles "Avangard," "Aleksandra Nazadze," "Anna Karenina," "Belyi Parus," "Exprompt," and "Juri Gagarin" to mention a few.

Rodionenko reports that one of his former students, A. Amechin, grows Japanese irises successfully in the southern Ukraine near Lvov and another, L. Mironova, in the vicinity of Vladivostok.

Edmundas Kondratas of Kaunas, Lithuania, reports that in that part of the USSR Ana Grinjuviene received a few Japanese irises from Rodionenko in 1980 and obtained fifteen older varieties from Adler and some of the Chochua cultivars. He has used them for hybridizing but the resulting seedlings were so like their undistinguished parents that he has abandoned them and is now working with modern cultivars and seeds obtained from the United States and Canada with the goal of developing cultivars of modern type with superior winter hardiness.

United States

The Society for Japanese Irises started quite informally. In 1960 Eleanor Westmeyer had discussed with Bee Warburton the desirability of having a society concerned with Japanese irises similar to some already in existence for other members of the genus. At the American Iris Society Convention in 1961 they and C. A. Swearengen agreed that the effort to form such a society should be made. Letters were written to people thought to be interested in Japan irises inviting them to join and the society was launched. Bylaws were adopted and the society was formally listed as a section of the American Iris Society in the April 1963 AIS Bulletin.

The first officers were: C. A. Swearengen of Terre Haute, Indiana, President; Eleanor Westmeyer of Stamford, Connecticut, Vice President and Editor; Bee Warburton of Westborough, Massachusetts, Secretary and Publication Chairman; and A. H. Hazzard of Kalamazoo, Michigan, Treasurer.

The first issue of *The Review,* the society's journal, was published in January 1964 under the editorship of Eleanor Westmeyer. She continued as editor for the first three volumes. William E. Ouweneel then accepted that responsibility and continued for eighteen years, 1967 through 1984, when Leland M. Welsh became editor.

The Review is published twice yearly, spring and fall. In addition to presenting cultural and varietal information of value to the advanced grower as well as to the beginner, *The Review* serves to keep members informed of the society's affairs and of happenings related to Japanese irises throughout the world. Other projects of the society are the partial subsidy of this book and the publication of a membership list and checklists of Japanese iris registrations and introductions. These lists are published periodically and between new printings are kept up to date in *The Review*. The first checklist was compiled in 1967 covering registrations for 1950 through 1966. This list was updated in 1981, 1986, and 1988.

An important effort of the society has been to encourage interest in Japanese irises through shows and garden tours. The first Japanese iris show of record in the United States was staged in Kalamazoo, Michigan, by the Southwestern Michigan Iris Society on July 6, 1963 under the chairmanship of Arthur Hazzard. The first show sponsored by the Society for Japanese Irises was held three years later in Terre Haute, Indiana, combined with the first arranged tour to visit the gardens of Russell Isle, W. S. Ouweneel, Arlie Payne, and C. A. Swearengen in that city, certainly at that time the Japanese iris center of the country. In later years similar garden visits were included as part of the shows in Summerville, South Carolina, Kalamazoo, Michigan, and elsewhere. In 1985 a "Japanese Iris Weekend" in Kalamazoo led to the decision to recognize these gatherings as Japanese Iris Conventions and to hold them annually. Such conventions are particularly important in the case of Japanese irises because, although section meetings devoted to them are part of the annual conventions of the American Iris Society, since the conventions are scheduled for peak bloom of the tall bearded irises Japanese irises are not seen in the garden tours.

Arlie Payne presented a silver cup to the society in 1966 to be awarded annually to the originator of the Japanese iris receiving that year the largest number of votes from American Iris Society judges. Known as the Payne Award it is currently the highest award that has been given to a Japanese iris in the United States.

Because of the wide scattering of members all over the United States, Canada, and other countries, only two meetings of the board and of the members can normally be held each year, at the time of the American Iris Society Convention and at the annual Japanese Iris Convention. Hence much of the business of the society is carried out by the board through correspondence and through the various committees such as those concerned with membership, publicity, slides, and a display garden program. Material of historical interest available for study by members on request is collected and maintained by the Historian-Librarian.

The presidents of the Society since its founding have been: C. A. Swearengen, 1964–66; Eleanor Westmeyer, 1967–72; Lorena M. Reid, 1973–74; Thornton M. Abell, 1975–78; Adolph J. Vogt, 1979–spring 1982; Virginia Burton, fall 1982–85; Currier McEwen, 1985–86; Donald Delmez, 1987–88 and Clarence E. Mahan, 1989–.

APPENDIX B ❧ *Where to See Japanese Irises*

United States Gardens

This list includes all the gardens listed in 1989 as display gardens by the Society for Japanese Irises, and a few others not yet so listed.

In addition to the name and address, the telephone number is shown so that a prospective visitor can phone in advance to select a mutually convenient time. Given in parentheses are the dates when the bloom is best for that garden. In the following list, the individual gardens are shown in a roughly geographic fashion.

New England

Dr. and Mrs. Currier McEwen
Seaways Gardens
RD 1, Box 818
South Harpswell, ME 04079
Phone (207) 833–5438
(July 7–21)

Shirley Pope
Pope's Perennials
39 Highland Avenue
Gorham, ME 04038
Phone (207) 839–3054
(mid-July)

Mr. and Mrs. John W. White
RRD 2, Box 980
Auburn, ME 04210
Phone (207) 345–9532
(mid to late July)

Mid-Atlantic

William L. Ackerman
18621 Mink Hollow Road
Ashton, MD 20861
Phone (301) 774–7538
(June 13–20)

George C. Bush
1739 Memory Lane Ext.
York, PA 17402
Phone (717) 755–0557
(mid-June to mid-July)

Mr. and Mrs. Sterling V. Innerst
2700A Oakland Road
Dover, PA 17315
Phone (717) 764–0281
(June 6–July 10)

Mr. and Mrs. Clarence Mahan
The Iris Pond
7311 Churchill Road
McLean, VA 22101
Phone (703) 873–8526
(June 1–July 7)

Presby Memorial Iris Gardens
474 Upper Mountain Road
Upper Montclair, NJ 07043
Phone (201) 783–5974
(early July)

Mrs. Andrew C. Warner
16815 Falls Road
Uppercoe, MD 21153
Phone (301) 374–4788
(June 15–30)

Nicholls Gardens
4724 Angus Drive
Gainsville, VA 22065
Phone (703) 754–9623
(June 14–24)

Southeast

Mrs. Wells E. Burton
3275 Miller Drive
Ladson, SC 29456
Phone (803) 873–7388
(mid-May–June 7)

East Central

Ensata Gardens
9823 E. Michigan Aenue
Galesburg, MI 49083
Phone (616) 668–7500
(first week in July)

Jill and Jim Copeland
34165 CR 652
Mattawan, MI 49071
Phone (616) 668–2156
(first two weeks of July)

Old Douglas Perennials
Anna Mae Miller
6065 Old Douglas Rd.
(N. 18th Street)
Kalamazoo, MI 49007
Phone (616) 349–5934
(June 29–July 12)

Shook Iris Garden
3907 Lincoln Lake Road
Lowell, MI 49331
Phone (616) 897–9169
(July 1–15)

Harold L. Stahly
8343 Manchester Drive
Grand Blanc, MI 48439
Phone (313) 694–7139
(June 6–July 8)

Rain Tree Garden
Jean Stallcop
RR7 Box 676
Greencastle, IN 46135
Phone (317) 672–8206
(June 15–25)

Florence Stout
150 North Main
Lombard, IL 60148
Phone (312) 627–1421
(July 1–7)

Adolph J. Vogt
5101 Fegenbush Lane
Louisville, KY 40218
Phone (502) 499–0024
(June 10–16)

Redbud Lane Iris Garden
Jerry and Melody Wilhoit
Rt. 1 Box 141
Kansas, IL 61933
Phone (217) 948–5478
(June 10–30)

Pacific Northwest

Aitken's Salmon Creek Garden
608 NW 119 Street
Vancouver, WA 98685
Phone (206) 573-4472
(mid-June)

Laurie's Garden
41886 McKenzie Hwy.
Springfield, OR 97478
Phone (503) 896-3756
(June)

Caprice Farm Nursery
15425 SW Pleasant Hill Rd.
Sherwood, OR 87140
Phone (503) 625-7241
(July 1-15)

California

Champions Nursery
12420, 7th Street
Yacaipa, CA 92399
Phone (719) 797-9381
(May 20-June 30)

Melrose Gardens
309 Best Road South
Stockton, CA 95205
Phone (209) 465-8578
(May 20-June 10)

West Central

Delmez Gardens
3240 Connecticut
St. Charles, MO 63301
Phone (314) 724-4274
(mid-June)

Calvin H. Helsley
Box 306
Mainsfield, MO 65704
Phone (417) 924-8380
(early to mid-June)

Pleasure Iris Gardens
425 E. Luna
Chaparral, NM 88021
Phone (505) 824-4299
(June 1-15)

Gardens in Japan

We are indebted to Mototeru Kamo and to the late Suichi Hirao for the following list of gardens in Japan and for the Japanese nurseries in the list of sources of Japanese irises. They both emphasize that this is a very incomplete listing. There are many other gardens where beautiful displays can be seen. The gardens are listed roughly geographically from north to south.

Kuribayashi Shobu En (garden in
  a school)
2-14 Hakkagakuen Tsukisamu
  Higashi
Sapporo 061-01
(mid to late July)

Tsukisami Iris Garden
Mr. Teikichi Ishiyama
12 Higashi-Ichijo Toyohiro,
  Tsukisamu
Sapporo, Hakkaido
(July)

Risokyo (private)
Torigamori Hukamochi
Towada Aomiri 034-01
(July)

Nagai Ayame Koen (park)
Miya Nagai, Yamagata Prefecture
Honshu 993
(early to mid-July)

Motsuji (temple)
Hiraizumi Iwate-Ken 029–41
(late June to mid-July)

Meiji Jingu (Meiji Shrine)
  Iris Garden
1–2 Shinen Yoyogi
Shibuya-ku Tokyo 151
(mid to late June)

Horikiri Shobuen (park)
2–19–1 Horikiri Katsushika-Ku
Tokyo 124
(June)

Keio Kyakkaen (private)
4–38–1 Tamagawa Chohu-Shi
Tokyo 182
(June)

Kamo Hanashobu En (nursery)
Harasato Kakegawa
Shizuoka 436–01
(late May to late June)

Hamamatsu Flower Park
195 Kanzanji Hamamatsu
Shizuoka 431–12
(June)

Udatsuyama Hanashobuen (park)
1–1–1 Hirosaka Kanazawa
Ishikawa 920
(mid to late June)

Takitani Hanashobu En (private)
Takitani Murou Uda Nara 633–03
(mid to late June)

Banshu Yamazaki Hanashobu En
  (private)
Yamazaki-Cho Shishiawa
Hyogo 671–25
(June)

Eitakuji Hanashobu En (private)
Eitakuji Santa Hyogo 669–23
(early July)

Ichihazama Shobuen
Sannou Shiseki Koen
Ichi-hazama, Kurihara
Miyagi 987–23
(late June)

Sawara Suisei Shokubutsuen
1837–2 Ogishima Sawara
Chiba 287
(June)

Shirokita Park
3–29–1 Ikue
Asahiku, Oosaka
(mid-June)

APPENDIX C ❧ *Sources of Japanese Irises*

United States Sources

This list of nurseries where one can obtain Japanese irises is incomplete but includes those that we know offer a good selection of modern varieties. A few nurseries in Japan are included also. For the United States nurseries a note is added as to whether they offer only their own introductions, a general list or both. The gardens are listed alphabetically. Those that specialize in Japanese irises are marked with an asterisk.

*William L. Ackerman
18621 Mink Hollow Rd.
Ashton, MD 20861
Own introductions only.

*Aitken's Salmon Creek Garden
608 NW 119th Street
Vancouver, WA 98665
Own introductions and general list

*George C. Bush
1739 Memory Lane Ext.
York, PA 17402
Own introductions and general list

*Caprice Farm Nursery, Inc.
15425 SW Pleasant Hill Road
Sherwood, OR 97140
Own introductions and general list

*Champions Nursery
12420 7th Street
Yacaipa, CA 92399
Own introductions and general list

*Delmez Gardens
3240 Connecticut St.
St. Charles, MO 63301
General list

*Ensata Gardens
9823 E. Michigan Ave.
Galesburg, MI 49053
Own introductions and general list

*The Iris Pond
7311 Church Hill Road
McLelan, VA 22101
Own introductions and general list

*Laurie's Gardens
41886 McKenzie Hwy.
Springfield, OR 97478
Own introductions and general list

*Melrose Gardens
309 Best Road South
Stockton, CA 95203
Own current introductions only

*Nichols Gardens
4724 Angus Drive
Gainesville, VA 22065
General list and William Ackerman's
     introductions

*Old Douglas Perennials
6065 Old Douglas Road
Kalamazoo, MI 49007
Own introductions and general list

Pleasure Iris Gardens
425 E. Luna
Chaparral, NM 88021
General list

*Popes Perennials
39 Highland Ave
Gorham, ME 04038
Introductions of Currier McEwen
     (Seaways Gardens) only

*Rain Tree Garden
RR2 Box 676
Greencastle, IN 46135
General list

*Redbud Lane Iris Garden
Rt. 1, Box 141
Kansas, IL 61933
General list

*Shook Iris Garden
3987 Lincoln Lake Road
Lowell, MI 49331
Own introductions and general list

Tranquil Lake Nursery
45 River Street
Rehobeth, MA 02769
General list

*Carol Warner
16815 Falls Road
Uppercoe, MD 21155
General list (no catalog)

White Flower Farm
Litchfield, CT 06759–0050
General list

Iris Nurseries in Japan

Almost all of the larger gardens in Japan sell plants but very few export them. This is due partly to language difficulties and partly to the expense and inconvenience involved in arranging for phytosanitary inspection. Four nurseries that will export are listed below. Any letters to these nurseries should be typed as the owners may not read English script.

Kamo Nurseries
Harasato Kakegawa
Shizuoka 436–01
FAX 0537–26–1213

Japanese Iris Nurseries
Miike Engei Kenkyujo (specializes in
     pot culture)
Mr. Nobuyuki Miike
260 Kushihashi
Isehara Kanagawa 259–1

Shuhoen Nurseries (specializes in
     Higo strain)
3–10–21 Okamura
Isago Yokahama 235

Mr. Teikichi Ishiyama
12 Higashi-Ichijo Toyohira
Tsukisamu Supporo 061–01

❧ *Contemporary Hybridizers*

United States

In the following list are shown the names and addresses of currently active U.S. hybridizers named in chronological order based on approximately when their hybridizing interests began. We apologize for any omissions.

Jonnye Rich
8501 Sunrise Ave.
Roseville, CA 95661

George C. Bush
1739 Memory Lane Ext.
York, PA 17402

Ben R. Hager
309 Best Road South
Stockton, CA 95205

Dr. Currier McEwen
RD 1 Box 818
South Harpswell, ME 04079

Dr. William L. Ackerman
P.O. Box 120
Ashton, MD 20861

Adolph Vogt
5101 Fegenbush Lane
Louisville, KY 40218

Mrs. Lorena M. Reid
41886 McKenzie Hwy.
Springfield, OR 97478

Mrs. F. W. Warburton
2 Warburton Lane
Westborough, MA 01581

Sterling V. Innerst
2700A Oakland Road
Dover, PA 17315

Jill Copeland, Jimmy Copeland
34165 CR 652
Mattawan, MI 49071

James W. Shook
3987 Lincoln Lake Road
Lowell, MI 49331

Terry Aitken
608 NW 119th St.
Vancouver, WA 98685

Mrs. Mark A. Dienstbach
2 Lake James Ct.
Florissant, MO 63034

Mrs. Ronald F. Miller
6065 Old Douglas Road
Kalamazoo, MI 49007

Robert A. Bauer and John A. Coble
Ensata Gardens
9823 E. Michigan Ave.
Galesburg, MI 49053

Donald Delmez
3240 Connecticut St.
Charles, MO 63301

John W. Wood
P.O. Box 861
Gaffney, SC 29342

Clarence E. Mahan
7311 Churchill Road
McLean, VA 22101

John W. White
RFD 2 Box 980
Auburn, ME 04210

Japan

We know that the following list, like that of hybridizers in the United States, is incomplete. We apologize for any omissions.

The list must start with the name of Dr. Shuichi Hirao, who died on June 8, 1988, but whose work continues through seedlings he did not live to see bloom and through the great influence his cultivars will continue to have for many years. His interests were very broad, including the Higo, Edo, and Ise strains, interspecific hybrids and tetraploids.

Dr. Koji Tomino, who specializes in Ises.

Yosho Mitsuda, working with Higos and one of the earliest breeders to develop polyploid cultivars.

Seiro Yoshie, who is particularly interested in very early Edo varieties.

Shigeo Oshida, whose interests embrace Edo and Higo Japanese irises and also *I. laevigata*.

Mototeru Kamo, working with Higos, Edos, interspecific hybrids and tetraploids.

Toyokayu Ichie, whose broad program includes Ises, Edos, Higos, interspecific hybrids and tetraploids.

Dr. Tsutoma Yabuya, actively engaged in research, especially the use of embryo culture and tetraploidy to develop fertile interspecific hybrids.

Hiroshi Shimizu, whose interests include Higos, Edos and tetraploidy.

APPENDIX E ❦ *Methods for the*
Induction of Tetraploidy

The general subject of tetraploidy has been discussed in Chapter 9. The methods for inducing the tetraploid or other polyploid states are presented here.

These methods are of three general types: the so-called clonal method using mature plants, the sprouted seedling method, and methods involving embryo culture. For details regarding the last the reader is referred to Yabuya (1985b). For the other two methods individual horticulturists and hybridizers have developed somewhat different techniques. The ones outlined here are those with which the author has had experience.

Clonal Method

In this method a plant about ½ to ⅝ inch in diameter at its base is cut off about ½ inch above the crown (where the leaves and rhizome meet) and a cup is scooped out of the remaining stump. The cup is made about ¼ inch deep so that its bottom is approximately ¼ inch above the meristem (the growing point of the plant). This cup is filled daily or every second day with an aqueous solution of 0.5% colchicine for three to five treatments. Soon new green shoots can be seen emerging from the stump around its border. Even at this stage one can soon have a fairly good idea of the success of the treatment because diploid shoots grow rapidly taller whereas polyploid ones remain stubby green growths for several weeks before they start to grow taller. Potted plants are best for the clonal method as the work can be done indoors under lights which are kept on 24 hours daily to encourage active growth. If the plant is growing in the ground it is essential to protect the stump from rain by covering it if rain threatens and scraping soil away somewhat so that the colchicine in the cup is not diluted by rain water.

Not infrequently the new growth emerging on one side of the cup may be diploid and that on the other side polyploid. If that occurs and both types live the result may be a sectorial chimera with the two different types of tissue persisting separately or the diploid tissue may overwhelm the polyploid part as the plant matures. The final result can be learned by examining the size of the pollen grains when the flower blooms as explained in the section on identification of tetraploids. Bloom may occur the following year but usually growth is so set back by the treatment that bloom is postponed.

Sprouted Seedling Method

In this method one starts with seeds harvested in the fall and kept at 34 to 40° F for one to six months as described in chapter 10. Any moldy or obviously nonviable seeds are discarded and the remainder are scattered over a moist sterile filter or blotting paper in sterile shallow covered dishes. For this purpose bacteriological dishes (Petri dishes) of 10 cm or larger size are ideal. The dishes, properly labeled as to the cross, are kept at about 70° F and a few drops of sterile water can be added from time to time to prevent the paper from becoming dry. Germination can be expected in one to four weeks. The first sign is the appearance of a small white protrusion, the hypocotyl. In a day or two the primitive root will appear as a white prolongation from the hypocotyl. A few days later a slit will be seen in the side of the hypocotyl and after another few days a tiny green shoot will emerge from the slit. When the green shoot is just visible, about ⅛ inch long, the seedling is ready to treat. The Petri dishes are examined each day and any seedlings ready for treatment are removed with forceps the tips of which have been sterilized by holding them a moment in a flame so as not to infect the seeds remaining in the Petri dish. Test tubes of suitable size or small jars are excellent to receive the seeds, using separate ones appropriately labeled for each cross. The test tubes or jars need not be sterile, for from that point on sterility is no longer necessary. When all the suitable seedlings have been placed in their tubes, enough colchicine solution is added to cover them well. For this a much weaker solution of colchicine is used than in the clonal method, 0.025% to 0.05%.

The seedlings remain in the solution 12 to 24 hours under lights and are then washed for several hours in gently running water and planted in a sterile germinating mix. As in the case of the clonal method, the unaffected seedlings start growing normally and the affected ones remain for weeks as short stubby sprouts. After two or three weeks many of the affected seedlings die. This is because the primitive root is especially affected by colchicine and becomes so altered that it cannot carry nutrients to the plant. For several weeks the little seedling is nourished by the endosperm of the seed. If the secondary roots from the base of the seedling form before the endosperm is exhausted the seedling survives and grows; if not it starves. About 10 to 20% of the treated seedlings live and of those perhaps 10 to 30% will be chimeras or, rarely, fully tetraploid, and the rest diploids. Hence one must start with one hundred or more seeds to have much chance of having useful polyploids.

Both methods require patience and perseverance and can be frustrating. Successful results with the clonal method result in a polyploid form of the same cultivar that was treated. Success with the sprouted seedling method gives new cultivars in polyploid (chimeral or fully tetraploid) form. Successful crosses of the polyploids obtained by either method will give either diploids or fully tetraploid seedlings depending on the degree of polyploidy of the parents, and no longer will there be chimeras that might, in time, revert to the diploid state.

Identification of Tetraploids

One can have an impression as to whether a treated plant is diploid or polyploid from its appearance. The polyploid tends to have stouter leaves of deeper green color and the flowers tend to be larger than those of diploids, with stronger substance. Further evidence may be seen in the anthers, which in the polyploid flowers are wider—although not much longer—than in diploids. The definitive decision is made by examining the pollen grains microscopically, for the tetraploid grains have roughly twice the volume of diploid grains. (Although the difference in size is fairly obvious, through the microscope they do not look twice as large because are seen in only two dimensions.) Determination of size is made much more accurate by using a small measuring lens in the eyepiece of the microscope. The technique is very simple. One merely takes an anther from the flower under study and dusts some pollen from it into a drop of water on a glass slide. A very high powered lens is not necessary: indeed, even an inexpensive grade-school microscope is perfectly adequate.

Examination of the pollen of a colchicine treated plant give information not only as to whether the plant is diploid or polyploid but also as to its degree of polyploidy. The cone-shaped growing part of the plant, the meristem, is made up of three layers; the outer one, layer one; the one beneath it, layer two; and the mass of cells filling in the rest of the cone, layer three. Layer one gives rise to the ectoderm (skin) of the plant and about a fifth of the reproductive cells (the pollen and ovules). Layer two provides the remaining four-fifths of the reproductive cells. Layer three gives rise to the general body (somatic) cells of the plant and contributes nothing to the reproductive cells. Thus, if all the pollen grains in the drop of water are of diploid size one knows that, for purposes of hybridizing, the plant is purely diploid, whereas if all are large it is tetraploid. If about a fifth of the pollen grains are of tetraploid size but most are smaller the plant is a chimera that is tetraploid in layer one and diploid in layer two. If however, most of the pollen is of tetraploid size the plant is diploid in layer one and tetraploid in layer two and, for purposes of hybridizing, will be very nearly as useful as a full tetraploid.

Having a chromosome count made on the colchicine-treated plant is not only unnecessary but can be misleading. Root tips, which are usually used for doing a chromosome count, come from layer three, and so tell nothing about the degree of polyploidy of the reproductive cells unless, which is rather rare, the treated plant is fully tetraploid in all three layers. A chromosome count does not identify chimeras that are useful in making crosses. However, to test a possible tetraploid of advanced generation, a root-tip chromosome count is informative, for since such a plant must be fully tetraploid, all the cells including those from layer three will be tetraploid if the plant has been successfully converted.

Further details about tetraploidy and methods of inducing it are provided in Griesbach et al. 1965, Arisumi 1964, and McEwen 1966, 1976.

❧ *Glossary*

Pronunciation is shown for some Japanese and botanical terms. Our authorities for the Japanese words are Akira Horinaka, Mototeru Kamo, and Clarence Maham. Pronunciation shown for botanical terms is based on that accepted by *Webster's Third International Dictionary Unabridged*.

Acid soil: Soil having an acid reaction, i.e., with pH lower than 7 (neutral), usually from 5 to 6.8. The lower the pH the greater the acidity.

Alkaline soil: Soil having an alkaline reaction, i.e., with pH above 7 (neutral). The higher the pH the greater the alkalinity.

Allele: (*ah léel*) One of a pair or series of forms of a gene of which only one is normally expressed, because they are situated at the same location in like chromosomes.

Allopolyploid (alloploid): A polyploid in which one or more sets of chromosomes come from different species.

Allotetraploid: A tetraploid alloploid.

Amoena: (*ah mé nu*t) An iris flower with white standards and colored falls.

Amphydiploid: A hybrid between two species that has at least one complete set of chromosomes derived from each parent species.

Anther: The pollen-bearing structure at the end of the stamen.

Anthocyanin: The primary cell-sap pigment of iris flowers. The most common form in irises produces the blue to purple and red colors.

Apogon: (*át pope gon*dola) Rhizomatous irises with no beard or crest.

Autopolyploid (autoploid): A polyploid having more than two sets of homologous chromosomes.

Ayame: (*áh ya*tch *met*) Ancient name in Japan for both *Acorus calamus* and Japanese irises but now used for *Iris sanguinea*.

Bicolor: A flower having standards and/or styles and falls of different colors.

Bitone: A flower having standards and/or styles and falls of different shades of the same color.

Bract: Also called spathe. A pointed, upright, leaf-like structure growing from the stalk below the flowers (see figures 13 and 14).

Branch: An offshoot from the stalk bearing one or more flower buds at its end.

Capsule: Also called pod. The round or oval body that develops from the ovary after fertilization and contains the seeds.

Carotenoids: Fat-soluble pigments including carotenes (yellows and orange), xanthophylls (yellow), and lycopenes (pink to red).

Chimera: (*kite mírror ah*) A plant that is partly diploid and partly polyploid.

Chlorosis: Yellowing of leaves due to loss or reduction of chlorophyll caused chiefly by deficiencies of iron, but also by deficiencies of magnesium, boron, or manganese.

Chlorophyll: The green pigment of plants, necessary for photosynthesis.

Chromosomes: Microscopically visible bodies within the nuclei of cells which contain the genes controlling hereditary characteristics of progeny. Their number is constant and characteristic for each species and cultivar. (*See* N number.)

Clone: One of a group genetically identical individuals resulting from vegetative multiplication of a single plant.

Colchicine: An alkaloid substance obtained from the autumn crocus (*Colchicum autumnale*) used to induce chromosome doubling in plants.

Continuing bloomer: A cultivar that sends up successive bloom stalks for an extended period without an intervening period when no new bloom stalks are seen. (*See* Repeater and Extended floral bloom.)

Crimped: Having fine folds or pleats at the edges of falls and standards.

Cross pollination: Placing the pollen of one flower on the stigma of a genetically dissimilar flower to fertilize it; often called "crossing."

Cultivar: A group of genetically identical plants maintained in cultivation for ornamental or utilitarian purposes. They are identified with names in a modern language, for instance, Iris "Immaculate Glitter." In general garden usage the term variety is also commonly used. (*See* Variety).

Cytogenetics: The study of the genetic features of cells, particularly of chromosomes and genes.

Dehisce: (*deed híss*) To open naturally and expose pollen, used of the mature anther and of the seed pod.

Diamond-dusted: Having a petal texture characterized by tiny glistening highlights.

Diploid: Having two sets of chromosomes in each somatic cell, one set contributed by each parent. Most plants occurring in nature are diploid.

Division: A single rhizome of a plant with its roots and fan of leaves. Also the act of dividing a clump into smaller parts.

DNA: Abbreviation for deoxyribonucleic acid, the chemical substance within chromosomes which controls genetic features and the production of new plant tissues.

Dominance: The quality of one of a pair or series of interacting genes to mask or suppress the expression of others at the same location. (*See* Recessive.)

Durability: The ability of a flower to withstand sun, wind, rain and other adverse conditions and to look fresh a normal number of days.

Edo: (*édit oh*) Old name of Tokyo; used, starting about 1920, to refer to all the Japanese irises developed over the centuries of collecting and hybridizing prior to the time of the Ise and Higo cultivars.

Egg: The female gamete (germ cell) located in the embryo sac of the ovule.

Embryo: The rudimentary plant within the seed.

Endosperm: A tissue containing stored food surrounding the embryo and nourishing it in the early period after germination until the roots can take over that function.

Ensata: (*end sága testament*) *Iris ensata,* the botanical name of the species Japanese iris.

Eupogon: (*yóu pope gon*dola) True bearded; a true bearded iris.

Extended floral bloom: The capacity of the individual flowers of some cultivars to bloom for longer than the usual number of days. In the case of Japanese irises this is four to five days instead of the usual two to three.

F_1: The first seedling generation of a cross.

F_2: The second successive generation obtained by self-fertilization or crossing among the F_1 individuals.

Falls: The three downward arching or flaring segments of the single Japanese iris flower, botanically the sepals, in contrast to the standards which, botanically, are the petals. In double flowers all six segments, sepals and petals, are falls.

Fan: A single set of leaves rising from the rhizome.

Fertilization: The union of the sperm and egg resulting in the embryo which becomes the new seedling.

Filament: The stalk of the stamen.

Form: As used in this book, the shape of the flower; also, a botanical variant.

Fungicide: An agent, usually chemical, that destroys fungi.

Fungus: Saprophytic or parasitic plants that reproduce from spores and by vegetative means. Of the many microscopic fungi in soil, some are harmless or beneficial, others cause molds, mildews, rusts, and botrytis rot.

Gamete: The male or female germ cell of an organism capable of sexual reproduction.

Gene: A unit of heredity. A portion of DNA of a chromosome capable of controlling one or more characteristics.

Gene pool: All the alleles of all the genes in a population.

Genotype: The sum total of all the genes present in an individual, as contrasted with phenotype.

Genus (plural genera): The taxonomic subdivision between family and species including several further subdivisions (subgenus, section, subsection, series, subseries).

Germination: The sprouting of seeds.

Grubs: Wormlike larvae of insects, such as beetles, usually found underground.

Haft: The narrower part of the falls and standards toward the center of the flower where they attach to the perianthe tube.

Halo: An area surrounding the signals of some cultivars that differs in color from what of the rest of the fall.

Hanashōbu: (*hót not shów uh book*) The Japanese word for Japanese irises (*Iris ensata*).

Heredity: The sum of the qualities and potentialities genetically derived from ancestors; transmission of qualities from ancestors to descendants.

Heterozygous (noun form, heterozygote): Having genes governing different inherited characteristics occupying one or more corresponding locations on like chromosomes so that the organism produces genetically variable progeny. (*See* homozygous.)

Hexaploid: Having six sets of chromosomes.

Higo: (*hé go*) The group name for the type of Japanese irises that began to be developed after about 1850 in the old province of Higo corresponding to the present Kumamoto Prefecture.

Homozygous (noun form, homozygote): Having genes governing the same inherited characteristics occupying one or more corresponding locations on like chromosomes so that the organism produces genetically like progeny.

Hue: Color; the distinctive characteristics of a color that enable it to be assigned a position in the spectrum.

Hybrid: A plant (or animal) resulting from a cross of genetically unlike parents, such as those of different species, or of offspring of previous interspecies crosses.

Hybridization: The act of pollinating flowers to produce hybrids. Used loosely, however, to refer to all pollination.

In vitro: In an artificial environment outside the living body.

In vivo: Within the living body of a plant or animal.

Inbreeding: Repeated selfing or crossing of siblings or related plants.

Inhibitor: In genetic usage a gene that inhibits the action of another gene. In more general use, a factor such as an enzyme or other substance that can prevent or delay an action from occurring.

Intermediates: Plants with flowers and heights between those of the miniatures (dwarfs) and those of usual size. Specific measurements have not been established for Japanese irises but those so referred to have flowers 4 to 5 inches in diameter on stalks 24 to 30 inches tall.

Interspecific cross: A cross of two plants from different species.

Intraspecific cross: A cross of two plants of the same species.

Introduce: To make a formal offering of an officially registered plant for sale, as through an advertisement.

Introduction: A cultivar offered for sale for the first time.

Ise: (*éat set*) A group name for the type of Japanese irises developed in Japan in the Ise-Matsuzaka district of central Honshu beginning around 1800, for which the name Ise-type began to be used about 1910.

Laevigata: (*lay* v*i*ctor *gó*t test*a*ment) Botanical name of the species *Iris laevigata* and the series *Laevigatae* which includes *I. laevigata, I. ensata, pseudacorus versicolor* and *virginica*.

Larva: The early, free-living form of an animal that changes structure markedly when it becomes an adult—for example, the caterpillar is the larva of a butterfly.

Leaf: The blade-like structure rising from the rhizome especially adapted for photosynthesis and transpiration. Collectively leaves are called foliage.

Linkage: Genetically the tendency for two or more genes to be inherited together as a unit due to their close location on the same chromosome.

Matte: A flat texture, as opposed to glossy, velvety, or diamond-dusted.

Meiosis: The process of division of the germ cells (eggs and pollen) by which the number of chromosomes is halved, giving each germ cell in diploids a single set of chromosomes (1N) instead of the 2N number of the somatic cells.

Meristem: The growing part of the plant; the undifferentiated plant tissue from which new cells arise.

Metaphase: The stage of mitosis at which the chromosomes are arranged in disk-like formation at the center of the nucleus and each one divides in preparation for the separation of their two halves to produce daughter cells, each of which has the original number of chromosomes.

Miniature: A small flower on a slender stalk of appropriate height. No specific measurements have been established for Japanese irises but in general those that have been so referred to have flowers about 4 inches in diameter on stalks 10 to 18 inches tall.

Mitosis: The process of cell division of the somatic cells by which each daughter cell has the same number (2N) of chromosomes as the cell from which they came.

Mulch: A covering for the soil, used to hinder evaporation, protect plant roots from winter injury, prevent plants from heaving in winter, preserve soil texture, keep down weeds, protect fruit and flowers from mud spattering, add organic matter to the soil, keep soil cool in summer, and make dry paths in winter. Salt hay, oat straw, leaves, sawdust, and many other natural materials fulfill all or some of these purposes. Plastic and aluminum sheeting are also used.

Mutant: A plant in which a chemical change in DNA has occurred or has been induced by such means as radioactive irradiation.

Mycoplasms or mycoplasmalike organisms: Microorganisms resembling bacteria but lacking true cell walls. Some species cause diseases in humans and other animals and in plants. Recently shown to be the cause of scorch in irises.

N number: Abbreviation used for the number of sets of chromosomes in a cell: 1N for the set of 12 chromosomes in the germ cells of Japanese iris (1N = 12); 2N for the two sets totaling 24 in the somatic cells of diploids (2N = 24), 4N for the four sets totaling 48 in the somatic cells of tetraploids, and so on.

Nematode: Any member of a phylum of non-segmented worms many of which are parasites of animals and plants. All concerned with plants are microscopic; some are harmful but many are harmless or useful.

Nucleus (plural nuclei): The large, roughly circular body within the cell that contains the chromosomes.

Ovary: The ovule-bearing structure at the base of the flower which after fertilization develops into the seed pod.

Ovules: Egg-containing structures in the ovary which, after fertilization, develop into seeds.

Parasite: A plant or animal that lives in or on an individual of another species without advantage to the host and usually doing it harm.

Pathogen: An organism that causes disease such as a virus, bacterium, or fungus.

Pendent: Hanging. Used to describe falls which hang. Often construed as derogatory, but many pendent falls are graceful.

Perianth tube: The slender tube connecting the ovary with the floral parts.

Perianth: In iris flowers, collective terms for standards and falls.

Pesticide: Any material used to kill pests—usually insects.

Petal: One of the inner series of perianth parts (standards) of the iris flower.

pH: A symbol used in chemistry to denote the relative concentration of hydrogen ions in a solution, hence a measure of acidity and alkalinity. Values of pH range from 0 to 14 on a logarithmic scale. A pH of 7 is neutral. Numbers below 7 indicate acidity and the lower the pH the greater the acidity. Numbers above 7 indicate alkalinity. Most soils are between 4 and 8 on the pH scale.

Phenotype: The physical appearance of an organism as contrasted to its genotype (genetic make-up).

Phylogeny: The evolutionary history of a species or other taxonomic unit.

Pistil: The female reproductive structures of a flower. In irises it consists of ovary, style, style branch, and stigma.

Plicata: A genetically controlled pattern of stitched and dotted edges of white or light colored falls in bearded irises. There are no true plicatas among Japanese irises but some edged or rimmed ones resemble that pattern.

Pod parent: The female parent, the one on which the seed pod will form.

Pogon: Bearded.

Pollen parent: The plant from the flower of which pollen is taken for the cross; the male parent.

Polyploid: A plant with cells having more than two complete sets of chromosomes.

Pseudacorus: (*pseudo óccupy ah rust*) Botanical name of the "yellow water iris," *Iris pseudacorus* which, like *Iris ensata,* is a species of series *Laevigatae*.

Pupa: Any insect in the nonfeeding stage of its development between the last larval and adult forms; often enclosed in a cocoon or shell-like structure.

Rebloom: A second period of bloom occurring in the late summer or fall several months after first bloom. Characteristic of bearded irises. (*See* Repeat.)

Rebloomer: A plant that reblooms.

Recessive: Having the quality characteristic of one of a pair or series of interacting genes to be masked or suppressed by the expression of others at the same location. (*See* dominance.)

Register: To record the name and description of an iris with the registrar of the American Iris Society.

Registration: A plant named and officially registered by the registrar of the American Iris Society.

Repeat bloom: A second period of bloom occurring only one to three weeks after the end of the first period of bloom. Characteristic of Japanese and Siberian irises. (*See* Rebloom.)

Repeater or repeat bloomer: A plant that repeats. These are of three types: occasional repeaters, in which repeat bloom usually is scant and does not occur every year; reliable repeaters which repeat suitably each year if growing well; and preferential repeaters in which performance at second bloom is better than at first. (*See* continuing bloomer.)

Rhizome: The fleshy tuberlike underground part of the iris plant. It is a modified type of stem with the roots emerging from underneath and the leaves and bloom stalks from the top.

Roots: The extensions of the plant below ground serving to absorb and conduct water and minerals. They also anchor the plant. In irises roots arise from the rhizome.

Scape: Same as stalk.

Sclerotia: A dormant stage in certain fungi consisting of black or reddish-brown small, hard bodies.

Seed pod or capsule: The elongated, round structure which develops from the ovary following fertilization and contains the seeds.

Self: A flower with all segments the same color except for the signals.

Self-pollination: Pollinating a flower with its own pollen or that of a genetically identical flower; often called "selfing."

Sepals: The flower segments arising from the outer part of the perianth. In the single Japanese iris flower, the falls; in doubles the outer row of falls.

Series: In the classification of irises, the major subdivisions of a subsection. The Japanese iris *Iris ensata* is a member of series *Laevigata* of subsection *Apogon*.

Shade: The tone of a given color dependent on the amount of white or black mixed with it. (*See* Tint.)

Signal: The striking mark at the base of the falls of Japanese irises. The color is usually a bright yellow but some are green.

Somatic cell: A body cell, in contrast to a germ cell or gamete.

Spathe (Spathe valve): A bract or modified leaf enclosing a flower. They may be green, red, or purple and fleshy or dry and papery (scarious). In the iris they enclose the bud but are below the open flower. (*See* also Bract.)

Species: Defined in various ways but usually considered to be a group of organisms that interbreed and are distinguishable from others. Species are designated with binomials consisting of a generic name (Iris) the first letter of which is capitalized, and a specific epithet (*ensata*) in small letters and the whole name Latinized and italicized. For greater precision in scientific literature the binomial is followed by a name, initial or abbreviation identifying the botanist whose description gives authority to the binomial used. For example, *Iris ensata,* Thunb. (for Thunberg).

Spores: Reproductive bodies, usually single cells, produced by bacteria, fungi, and other lower plants. They are resistant to adverse conditions and can remain dormant for long periods.

Stalk: The upright stem which rises from the rhizome and bears the flowers.

Stamen: The male reproductive parts of the flower consisting of a filament having at its end the anther which bears the pollen grains.

Standards: Botanically the petals; the more or less upright segments that form the inner series of the perianth of which the flaring or drooping falls (the sepals) form the outer series. In Japanese irises only flowers of the single form have standards; in the double flowers the petals, like the sepals, are in the position of falls.

Stigma: The small liplike structure on the under (outer) surface of the style close to its end, on which pollen is deposited to effect fertilization.

Styles: The three firm, petallike structures rising from the center of the flower which are connected with the ovary and bear the stigmas.

Substance: The deep tissue (as distinguished from surface) characteristics of the falls and standards which determine their firmness or flexibility, and to a large extent the flower's form.

Systemic: A term applied to pesticides, including fungicides, which are absorbed by the plant without harm but are lethal to pests when they chew or suck sap from the plant. Systemic pesticides remain active longer than those of contact type and when used properly are less harmful to bees and other beneficial insects.

Tailored: Used of a flower which is not ruffled or crimped.

Taxon: Any one of the categories such as species, genus, class, order, or division into which living organisms are classified.

Taxonomy: The science of classification of organisms.

Terminal: The end of the stalk as distinct from its branches.

Tetraploid: Literally, fourfold; a plant having four sets of somatic chromosomes instead of the usual two sets. (*See* diploid.)

Texture: The surface characteristics of falls and standards.

Tint: A light tone of a given color depending on its admixture with varying amount of white.

Tone: The quality or value of a given color with reference to its darkness or lightness.

Triploid: A plant with three sets of somatic chromosomes. All are sterile. Although none has been recorded among Japanese irises theoretically one could result from crossing diploids with tetraploids.

Variety: Horticulturally, a group of individuals within a species differing sufficiently to be given a Latin varietal name usually preceded by the abbreviation var. In general garden usage the term is commonly used as synonymous with cultivar to refer to a particular cultivated plant. Cultivar is the preferred term but both, as in this book, are used interchangeably.

Versicolor: (*vérse sit color*) Botanical name of the wild blue flag of the northeastern United States; a species of series *Laevigatae*.

Virus: submicroscopic infective agent that reproduces only within cells and may cause diseases in plants and animals.

Wide cross: A cross between plants of different species, subseries, or series. They are not often successful, and the resulting seedlings are almost always sterile.

❧ References

Ackerman, W. L. 1973. Japanese iris with five-day bloom. *Amer. Hort.* 52(1):18–19.

——. 1987a. Breeding new types of Japanese iris. *The Review* 24(1):16–19.

——. 1987b. Breeding for dwarfness in Japanese iris. *The Review* 24(1):34–36.

——. 1988. Battling garden varmints. *The Review* 25: 32–34.

——. 1989. Personal communication.

Ackerman, W. L., and S. Bentz. 1986a. Inheritance of white flower color in Japanese iris. *The Review* 12(1):19–21.

——. 1986b. Pink color in Japanese iris. *The Review* 23(2): 25–28.

Ackerman, W. L., and M. Williams. 1981. Extending the blooming season and prolonging flower longevity of *Iris kaempferi*. *The Review* 18(1):1–3.

——. 1982. Japanese iris flowers with multiple parts beyond the normal sequence of threes. *Bull. Amer. Iris Soc.* 119 (1):22–27.

Aitken, T. 1987. Personal communication.

Arisumi, T. 1964. Colchicine—induced tetraploid and cytochimeral daylilies. *Jour. Heredity* 5:254–61; reprint, 1966. *Hemerocallis Jour.* 20:59–67.

Bald, J. G. 1969. Scorch disease of rhizomatons iris. Bull. Amer. Iris Soc. 195:26–30.

Bauer, R. 1986. Germination of Japanese and Siberian iris seeds. *The Review* 23(1):11–15.

——. 1989. J. I. culture in artificial bogs. *The Review* 26(1):24–25.

Blyth, B. 1988. Personal communication.

Burton, V. 1987. Personal communication.

Cameron, R. 1908. Iris laevigata (Kaempferi). *Horticulture* 8(5):131.

Coble, J. A. 1985. Galesburg garden culture. *The Review* 22(1):18–19.

——. 1987a. From pollination to bloom in two years. *Bull. Amer. Iris Soc.* 266:39–40; reprint 1978. *The Review* 24(2):21–22.

——. 1987b. Thrips and spider mites. *The Review* 24(2):37–39.

——. 1988. Personal communication.

Collins, J. 1978. Personal communication.

Craig, J. 1967. The pot culture of Japanese irises. *The Review* 4(1):3–4.

Danielson, H. 1984. Growing Japanese irises in New Mexico. *The Review* 21(2):41–43.

——. 1987. Personal communication.

Davidson, B. L. 1980. The paired species of irises III. *Bull. Amer. Iris Soc.* 237:22–26.

Delmez, D. 1986. The less than perfect garden culture. *The Review* 23(1):17–18.

——. 1989. Personal communication.

Dodge, B. O. 1946. Lesion nematodes on roots of Japanese iris. *Jour. New York Botanical Garden* 47(562):246–48.

Eigsti, O. J., and P. Dustin, Jr. 1955. *Colchicine in agriculture, medicine, biology and chemistry.* Ames: Iowa State College Press.

Faust, M. 1988. Personal communication.

Fisk, A. 1948. Notes on *Iris kaempferi. Brit. Iris Soc. Year Book.*

Flore de serres. 1874. *Flore de serres et de jardin de l'Europe* 20:2073–74.

Griesbach, R. A., O. W. Fay, and L. Horsfall. 1963. Induction of polyploidy in newly-germinated hemerocallis seedlings. *Hemerocallis Jour.* 17:70–75.

Gunther, W. J. 1976. Report from California. *The Review* 13(1):17–18.

———. 1987. Personal communication.

Hager, B. R. 1972. Nematodes in Japanese irises. *The Review* 9(2):16.

———. 1987. Japanese iris culture and problems. *Bull. Amer. Iris Soc.* 266:42–44.

———. 1989. Personal communication.

Harborne, J. B. 1988. Personal communication.

Hazzard, A. H. 1964. Growing and showing Japanese irises in the north. *The Review* 1(1):8.

Hewitt, J. 1987. Personal communication.

Hirao, S. 1963. Iris kaempferi (Japanese irises) in Japan with particular reference to their form. *Proceedings of the First International Symposium on Irises.* Florence: Società Italiana dell'Iris.

———. 1964. Pot culture of Japanese irises. *The Review* 1(3):36–38.

———. 1984. The Japanese iris in Japan. *The Review* 21(1):11–13.

———. 1987. Personal communication.

———. 1988. The Japanese iris: Its history, varieties and cultivars. *The Review* 25(2):38–46; reproduces English text of Kuribayashi and Hirao 1971.

Hollingworth, R. H. 1979. Botrytis rot of Siberian irises. *The Siberian Iris* 4(9):12–14.

Horinaka, A. 1987. Personal communication.

Ito, T. 1966. The culture of irises in Japan. *The Review* 3(1):5–14.

Jackson, R. S. 1972. Botrytis rhizome rot—a review. *Bull. Amer. Iris Soc.* 204:35–40.

Kamo, M. 1989. Personal communication.

Korcak, R. F. 1987. Iron deficiency chlorosis. In *Horticultural Reviews,* ed. J. Janick, 9, 133–86. New York: Van Nostrand Reinhold.

Kuribayashi, M., and S. Hirao. 1971. *The Japanese iris: Its history, varieties, and cultivars.* Tokyo: Published for The Japan Iris Society by Asahi Shimbun Publishing Co.

Lawrence, G. H. M. 1953. A reclassification of the *genus iris. Gentes Herb.* 8:346–71.

Love, F. 1988. Personal communication.

Loveridge, G. 1988. Personal communication.

Marschner, H. 1986. *Mineral nutrients of higher plants.* New York: Academic Press.

McEwen, C. 1966. Tetraploidy in Siberian irises. *British Iris Soc. Year Book.* 77–84.

———. 1971a. Efforts to induce tetraploidy in Japanese irises. *The Review* 8(1):9.

———. 1971b. Obtaining early maturity of seedlings in the north. *Bull. Amer. Iris Soc.* 203:65–66.

———. 1973. Factors influencing germination of Japanese iris seeds and health of the sprouted seedlings. *The Review* 10(2):4–6.

———. 1974. Factors influencing germination of Japanese iris seeds. *Bull. Amer. Iris Soc.* 213:32–36.

———. 1976. Methods of inducing tetraploidy in Siberian and Japanese irises. *Bull. Amer. Iris Soc.* 223:20–23.

———. 1978. Experience with *Pratylenchus penetrans*. *The Siberian Iris* 4(8):8–10.

———. 1979. Performance of Japanese irises in soils of different pH. *The Review* 16(2):1–4.

———. 1983. A choice of terms for remontancy in Siberian and Japanese irises. *The Siberian Iris* 5(7):8–9.

———. 1985. A question of disease in Japanese irises. *The Review* 22(1):20–24.

———. 1986a. Continuing, repeat and re-bloom. *The Review* 23(1):27–30.

———. 1986b. Some miscellaneous Japanese iris observations—1985. *The Review* 23(1):25–26.

———. 1988. Experience with seaweed and pineneedle mulches. *The Review* 25(2):31–32.

———. 1989. Personal experience.

Miller, A. M. 1986. When to divide Japanese irises (?) July (?)—Sept. (?) *The Review* 23(2):43.

Miller, A. M. 1986. Personal communication.

Miller, A. M., and R. A. Bauer. 1987. Edo, Higo or Ise: A short history of Japanese iris cultivation. *Bull. Amer. Iris Soc.* 266:10–12.

Naegale, J. A., and H. C. Fordham. 1978. Insect pests of irises. In *The world of irises*, ed. B. Warburton and M. Hamblen 350–54. Wichita, Kansas: The American Iris Society.

Nelson, K. 1989. How to register and introduce an iris. *Bull. Amer. Iris Soc.* 272:79.

Ouweneel, W. E. 1968. Kaempferi vs. ensata vs. laevigata. *The Review* 5(2):35–39.

———. 1969a. Kaempferi vs. ensata vs. laevigata, continued. *The Review* 6(2):10.

———. 1969b. Dr. George M. Reed. *The Review* 6(2):13–21.

———. 1972. Intensive care section. *The Review* 9(2):21.

———. 1977. Lesson '76. *The Review* 14(2):6–8.

———. 1981. Our readers write. *Bull Amer. Iris Soc.* 240:53–54.

Padgett, G. 1987. Japanese irises in Florida. *The Review* 24(2):33–34.

———. 1988. Japanese irises in Florida. *The Review* 25(2):35–36.

Payne, W. A. 1964. Judging the Japanese iris. *The Review* 1(2):21–26.

Porter, C. L. 1979. *Taxonomy of flowering plants*. 2d ed. San Francisco: W. H. Freeman and Co.

Reed, A. L. 1929. The significance of Japanese names for iris. *Bull. Amer. Iris Soc.* 32:13–20.

Reed, G. M. 1928. The Japanese iris. *Bull. Amer. Iris Soc.* 28:40–50.

———. 1931. The iris of Japan. *Bull. Amer. Iris Soc.* 40:3–48.

Rich, G. 1989. Personal communication.

Rodionenko, G. I. 1964. Wild iris species of the U.S.S.R. Brit. Iris Soc. Year Book, 117–18.

———. 1987. Personal communication.

Ross, J. 1978. Report from Huntesville, Alabama. *The Review* 15(1):7.

Schafer, M. 1989. New thoughts on pollination. *The Siberian Iris* 6(9):5–6.

Sjolund, R. D. 1989. Personal communication.

Sjolund, R. D., L. L. Stoll, K. G. Jensen, and G. Fang. 1989. Phloem limited mycoplasmalike organisms associated with iris scorch disease. In preparation.

Steiger, M. 1960. Zukunftziele bei der *Iris kaempferi*. *Jahrbuch der Deutsch. Iris-Gesellschaft*, 65–67.

———. 1963. Lime and drought resistant tetraploid *Iris kaempferi*. *Proceedings of the First International Symposium on Iris*. Florence: Società Italiana dell'Iris; reprint 1970. *The Review* 7(1):7–8.

————. 1964. Tetraploid *Iris kaempferi*. *The Review* 1(2):19–20.

Swearengen, C. A. 1964. Soil acidity and its comparative effect on plant growth. *The Review* 1(3):47.

Tamberg, T. 1985. Hybrids involving Siberian irises. *Bull. Amer. Iris Soc.* 258:30–33.

Tiffney, S. 1978. A new minor pest and what to do about it. *The Siberian Iris* 4(8):5–8.

Tilley, E. 1988. Personal communication.

Tomino, K. 1968. Studies of the *genus Iris* in Japan especially cytotaxonomy of the genus and breeding of *Iris ensata* Thunberg. *Bull. of the Lib. Arts Dept, Mei University* 28:1–59; reprinted from 1958. *The Review* 5(1):3–20.

Tomino, K., and O. Sakurai. 1972. Cross between *Iris pseudacorus* L. and *I. ensata* Thunb. *Bull Fac. Edu. Mei Univ.* 23:17–26 (in Japanese).

United States Department of Agriculture. 1960. Index of plant diseases in the United States: Agricultural handbook 165. Washington, D.C.: USDA.

Vogt, A. 1988. Personal communication.

Wadekamper, J. 1972. Scorch in irises. *Bull. Amer. Iris Soc.* 204:21–23.

————. 1987. Personal communication.

Warburton, B. 1988. Personal communication.

Weiler, J. H., 1978. Diseases in irises. In *The world of irises,* ed. B. Warburton and M. Hamblen. 342–48. Wichita, Kansas: The American Iris Society.

Welsh, L. M. 1983. Arthur H. Hazzard. *The Review* 20(1):2–4.

————. 1988. Judging Japanese irises. *The Review* 25(1):17–18.

Westmeyer, E. 1965. The classification of Japanese irises. *The Review* 2(1):7–11.

————. 1978. Hanashobu—the Japanese iris. In *The world of iris,* ed. B. Warburton and M. Hamblen, 255–64. Wichita, Kansas: The American Iris Society.

————. 1987. Personal communication.

Wong, S. I. 1987. Ikebana. Bull. Amer. Iris Soc. 266:55–61.

Wood, J. W. 1983. Extracts from letter from Dr. Shuichi Hirao to John W. Wood. *The Review* 20(1):4–5.

————. 1987a. Influence of pond culture. *Bull. Amer. Iris Soc.* 226:19.

————. 1987b. Growing Japanese irises in an alkaline environment. *Bull. Amer. Iris Soc.* 266:18.

Yabuya, T. 1983. Pollen storage of *Iris ensata* Thunb. in organic solvents and dry air under freezing. *Japan Jour. Breed.* 33:269–74.

————. 1984. Fundamental studies in the interspecies cross-breeding of *Iris ensata* Thunb. *Bull. Laboratory of Plant Breeding, Faculty of Agriculture, Miyazaki Univ.* 4. English summary 104–11.

————. 1985a. Cytogentical characteristics in F_1 hybrids of *Iris pseudacorus* L. × *I. ensata* Thunb. *Bull. Faculty of Agriculture, Miyazaki Univ.* 32:181–86.

————. 1985b. Amphidiploids between *Iris laevigata* Fisch. and *I. ensata* Thunb. induced through in vitro culture of embryos treated with colchicine. *Japan Jour. Breeding* 35:136–44.

————. 1987. High performance liquid chromatographic analysis of anthocyanims in induced amphidiploids of *Iris laevigata* Fisch. × *I. ensata* Thunb., *Euphytica* 36:381–83.

————. 1989. Personal communication.

Yabuya, T., and H. Yamagata. 1980. Elucidation of seed failure and breeding of F_1 hybrid in reciprocal crosses between *Iris ensata* Thunb. and *I. laevigata* Fisch. *Japan Jour. Breed.* 30(2):139–50.

❧ *Index*